COOKING WITH
Bon Appétit

COOKING WITH

Bon Appétit

Special Occasion Desserts

THE KNAPP PRESS
Publishers
Los Angeles

Published by The Knapp Press
5900 Wilshire Boulevard, Los Angeles, California 90036

Library of Congress Cataloging-in-Publication Data

Main entry under title:

Special occasion desserts.

  (Cooking with Bon appétit)
  Includes index.
  1. Desserts. I. Bon appétit. II. Series.
TX773.S74 1985   641.8′6   85-14659
ISBN 0-89535-170-6

On the cover: *Spiced Chocolate Torte Wrapped in Chocolate Ribbons*

Printed and bound in the United States of America

10   9   8   7   6   5   4   3

❦ Contents

🍒 Foreword

Styles in food, as in clothing, come and go. One year Tex-Mex is all the rage; the next year it's sushi bars. But no matter where the latest culinary trend is leading, fabulous desserts will never be out of favor for celebration dinners. A well-chosen dessert rounds out the menu, providing just the right counterpoint to the preceding courses. Cool mousses or fruit mixtures are refreshing grace notes after a heavy meal. A rich, satisfying cake or pastry, on the other hand, makes even the lightest repast seem a feast.

This collection of over 150 *Bon Appétit* recipes features desserts for every special occasion. There are soufflés and Bavarian creams that practically float off the plate, while on the more substantial side you will find warm sauced crepes, buttercream-filled tortes, handsome molded charlottes and a great assortment of unusual cheesecakes. Since the last thing a busy cook needs is eleventh-hour fussing, nearly all the recipes include do-ahead tips—so even the most spectacular desserts can be prepared one step at a time, well in advance of serving.

And spectacular is the word for this selection. Lavish desserts have long been a *Bon Appétit* trademark, and we have chosen the most stunning of all for inclusion here. There is something in every conceivable flavor from pears to peppermint, and especially noteworthy is the terrific array of chocolate specialties—gossamer chocolate mousses, fudgy chocolate-nut loaves, chocolate-filled cakes and meringues, frozen chocolate creams. . . . For the devoted chocophile, any one of them is reason enough for a party.

Surely there's a birthday or anniversary, a graduation or promotion coming up. Celebrate it! And make the occasion doubly memorable with one of these extraordinary finales.

1 ❦ Mousses, Bavarians and Soufflés

Choosing the dessert for a celebration dinner often provokes a dilemma: It must be beautiful and festive but not heavy. The perfect solution is a mousse, Bavarian or soufflé, all supremely elegant but light enough to complement the heartiest meal.

Mousses and Bavarians are very close relations. A classic Bavarian, or *bavarois*, always contains eggs and cream, both whipped to airy lightness, with gelatin added as a stabilizer. Mousse, which is French for "foam" or "froth," usually includes these same three ingredients, but not always; chocolate mousses, for example, are often firm enough without gelatin.

Though comparably ethereal, a soufflé is an altogether different creature. Whipped cream and gelatin don't enter the picture here. Instead, a thick sauce containing egg yolks—the soufflé base—is lightened with beaten egg whites and baked until puffy and browned. Though easy to make, soufflés have one foible that has earned them their reputation as prima donnas: They must be served the moment they emerge from the oven.

This selection of mousses, soufflés and such provides a generous sampling of their infinitely varied flavors. If you love exotic combinations, try Champagne Grapefruit Mousse Cake (page 2), Honey Hazelnut Mousse with Apricot Sauce (page 9), Lebkuchen Soufflé with Dark Beer Sabayon, even Fig Soufflé with Parmesan (both on page 19). For something simpler, choose from Lemon Bavarois, Mousse au Café (both on page 3), or one of the fabulous chocolate creations. No matter what else is on your menu, if it concludes with any of these desserts everyone is guaranteed to consider the meal very special indeed.

❧ Mousses and Bavarians

Champagne Grapefruit Mousse Cake

8 servings

½ cup Champagne
½ cup sugar
1½ tablespoons frozen grapefruit juice concentrate, thawed
24 ladyfingers

Mousse
1 cup Champagne
½ cup grapefruit juice
2 envelopes unflavored gelatin

Swiss Meringue
2 egg whites
6 tablespoons sugar

1 cup whipping cream
2 tablespoons sugar

Glaze
Juice of ½ grapefruit
1 tablespoon unflavored gelatin

1 cup whipping cream, room temperature
2 tablespoons sugar

Grapefruit sections and mint leaves (garnish)
Grapefruit Coulis*

Line 7- or 8-inch mold or fluted bowl with one large piece of plastic wrap.

Combine ½ cup Champagne with ½ cup sugar and grapefruit juice concentrate in medium bowl and blend well. Trim ladyfingers to ⅔ depth of mold or bowl (reserve small pieces). Line inside edge of mold with ladyfingers, rounded sides out. Brush ladyfingers generously with half of Champagne mixture.

For mousse: Combine ¼ cup Champagne, ¼ cup grapefruit juice and gelatin in small saucepan and let stand until gelatin has softened. Place over low heat and stir until gelatin has dissolved, then blend in remaining Champagne and grapefruit juice. Remove from heat and cool until slightly thickened (*do not refrigerate.*)

For Swiss meringue: Combine egg whites and sugar in large bowl of electric mixer. Set bowl over (not in) simmering water and whisk gently until mixture is hot to touch. Immediately transfer bowl to electric mixer and beat at next to highest speed until bowl is cool to touch, about 3 to 5 minutes.

Combine 1 cup cream and 2 tablespoons sugar in medium bowl and beat until soft peaks form. Gently whisk/fold mousse mixture into Swiss meringue; then whisk/fold in whipped cream. Half fill mold with mixture. Add single layer of ladyfingers, rounded side down. Brush ladyfingers with remaining Champagne mixture. Spoon enough remaining mousse mixture into mold to fill completely. Freeze at least 3 hours.

For glaze: Combine grapefruit juice and gelatin in small saucepan and let stand until gelatin is softened. Stir over low heat until gelatin is dissolved. Let cool completely (*do not refrigerate*).

Cut 8-inch circle from heavy cardboard. Unmold cake onto cardboard. Transfer to wire rack. Set rack on large baking sheet or platter.

Combine room temperature whipping cream with sugar in medium bowl and whisk briefly, just until mixture begins to thicken (it should still be quite liquid). Add cooled glaze mixture and blend well. Pour over entire surface of frozen cake, covering evenly and completely with thin layer (gelatin causes glaze to set up very quickly). Refrigerate cake until ready to serve.

Just before serving, decorate top of dessert with grapefruit sections and mint leaves. Serve with grapefruit coulis.

*Grapefruit Coulis

1 10-ounce jar apple jelly	8 ounces grapefruit sections

Combine apple jelly and grapefruit in blender and puree until smooth. Turn into bowl. Set aside at room temperature until ready to serve.

Lemon Bavarois

A refreshing party dessert from the Hotel Palácio dos Seteais in Sintra, Portugal.

20 servings

1 quart milk
Peel of 2 lemons (yellow part only)

3 tablespoons water
1 tablespoon fresh lemon juice
2 tablespoons unflavored gelatin

8 egg yolks

1 cup superfine sugar
Small pinch of salt

4 cups (1 quart) whipping cream
½ cup powdered sugar

Fresh fruit

Combine milk and peel in large saucepan and bring to simmer over medium-high heat. Remove from heat and let cool. Strain milk; discard lemon peel.

Blend water and lemon juice in cup. Sprinkle gelatin over top. Let stand until liquid is completely absorbed, about 5 minutes.

Combine yolks, sugar and salt in large bowl of electric mixer and beat until mixture is thick and forms slowly dissolving ribbon when beaters are lifted. Return milk to medium-high heat and bring to simmer. Slowly whisk hot milk into yolk mixture. Blend in gelatin. Place over medium heat and cook, stirring constantly, until custard coats spoon and registers 180°F on candy thermometer; *do not boil.* Transfer custard to large bowl and let cool.

Oil 3-quart ring mold. Combine cream and powdered sugar in another large bowl and whip until stiff. Fold into cooled custard. Turn into prepared mold, smoothing top. Cover with plastic wrap. Refrigerate mold until completely set, at least 2 hours.

To serve, dip mold briefly into warm water and pat dry. Carefully invert bavarois onto platter. Fill center with fresh fruit.

Mousse au Café

6 servings

3 eggs, separated
½ cup powdered sugar
1 envelope unflavored gelatin
¼ cup coffee liqueur
⅔ cup strong brewed coffee

Pinch of salt
2 tablespoons sugar
2 cups whipping cream
2 tablespoons coffee liqueur

Beat yolks in large bowl of electric mixer, adding powdered sugar gradually until mixture is pale yellow. Sprinkle gelatin over ¼ cup liqueur and let stand to soften. Heat coffee in small saucepan and whisk into yolks. Pour back into saucepan and cook over medium heat, whisking constantly, just until mixture simmers. Add gelatin and stir until thoroughly blended and dissolved. Set aside until cool and slightly thickened, stirring occasionally.

Beat whites with salt until soft peaks form. Slowly beat in sugar. Using same beaters, whip cream with 2 tablespoons liqueur until stiff. Fold meringue and whipped cream alternately into coffee mixture, beginning and ending with cream. Spoon into dessert dishes and chill thoroughly.

Almond Coffee Bavarian with Cognac Cream

8 servings

Bavarian

2 cups half and half
2½ ounces (½ cup) blanched almonds, toasted and coarsely chopped

1 tablespoon unflavored gelatin
⅓ cup cold water
4 eggs, separated
1 egg yolk
1 cup plus 1 tablespoon sugar
1 tablespoon plus 1 teaspoon Cognac
2¼ teaspoons instant coffee powder dissolved in 1 tablespoon warm water

2 teaspoons vanilla
¼ teaspoon almond extract
¾ cup whipping cream, beaten to stiff peaks
⅛ teaspoon cream of tartar

Cognac Cream

1½ cups whipping cream
4 tablespoons sugar
2 tablespoons Cognac
1 teaspoon vanilla

¾ cup sliced almonds, lightly toasted
Fresh strawberries

For bavarian: Combine half and half and almonds in heavy medium saucepan and bring to boil. Reduce heat and simmer 15 minutes.

Soften gelatin in cold water. Strain half and half into bowl, pressing on almonds with back of spoon to extract as much liquid as possible. Discard almonds. Off heat, whisk yolks and ½ cup sugar in double boiler until well blended. Gradually whisk in half and half. Set over simmering water and stir using wooden spoon until custard thickens enough to coat back of spoon and leaves path when finger is drawn across, about 10 minutes. Add gelatin and stir to dissolve. Remove from over water. Transfer to metal bowl. Set in larger bowl filled with water and ice. Stir until custard cools and begins to thicken. Blend in Cognac, coffee, vanilla and almond extract. Fold in whipped cream. Using clean, dry beaters, beat whites and cream of tartar until soft peaks form. Add remaining sugar 1 tablespoon at a time and beat until stiff but not dry. Fold into custard. Pour into 8-cup metal bowl with round bottom. Cover and refrigerate bavarian at least 1½ hours.

For cream: Beat cream and sugar to stiff peaks. Blend in Cognac and vanilla.

Dip base of bowl quickly in hot water. Wipe base dry. Unmold bavarian onto serving plate. Cover with ¾-inch-thick layer of Cognac cream. Sprinkle with almonds. Spoon remaining cream into pastry bag fitted with star tip. Pipe rosettes around base at 1½-inch intervals. Pipe 2 crisscross rows of rosettes atop bavarian. Set strawberries between rosettes. Refrigerate 30 minutes before serving.

Coffee and Cream Mousse

In this recipe, the cream is on top rather than in the mousse itself.

6 servings

1 envelope unflavored gelatin
¼ cup Irish whiskey or coffee liqueur
1¾ cups espresso or other strong coffee

3 egg yolks, room temperature
½ cup powdered sugar, sifted

1 teaspoon unflavored gelatin
2 tablespoons Irish whiskey or coffee liqueur

1 cup whipping cream
¼ cup powdered sugar, sifted
1 tablespoon grated sweet chocolate

Sprinkle 1 envelope gelatin over ¼ cup Irish whiskey and let stand 3 minutes to soften. Pour espresso into small saucepan, add softened gelatin and stir over low heat until gelatin is dissolved.

Beat egg yolks, gradually adding ½ cup powdered sugar, until mixture is thick and lemon colored and forms ribbon when dropped from beaters. Gradually beat in coffee mixture. Strain through sieve. Cover and refrigerate until slightly thickened, stirring occasionally. Divide among 6 goblets or Irish coffee glasses and chill until thick.

Sprinkle 1 teaspoon gelatin over 2 tablespoons whiskey and let stand 3 minutes to soften. Stir over hot water until gelatin is completely dissolved. Let cool to room temperature.

Whip cream with ¼ cup powdered sugar until soft peaks form. Slowly add cooled gelatin mixture and continue beating until stiff. Pipe through pastry bag or spoon over thickened coffee mousse. Refrigerate until firm. Just before serving, sprinkle each mousse with grated chocolate.

Le Chantilly

8 to 10 servings

Mocha Bavarian Cream
5 egg yolks
½ cup sugar
1 envelope unflavored gelatin
1½ cups milk

2 tablespoons coffee liqueur or water
1 ounce unsweetened chocolate, melted
2 teaspoons instant coffee powder

1 cup whipping cream

Decoration
1¼ cups whipping cream

2 ounces semisweet chocolate, broken into pieces
1 tablespoon coffee liqueur

For bavarian cream: Lightly oil 8-inch round cake pan. Beat yolks until thick and lemon colored, adding sugar gradually. Sprinkle gelatin over milk in pan. Bring to simmer, stirring constantly.

When milk is simmering, add a small amount to the yolks, stirring quickly to blend. Return mixture to saucepan and bring *just* to boil, whisking constantly. Remove from heat, stir in liqueur, melted chocolate and coffee powder and blend well. Let cool to room temperature, stirring occasionally.

Whip cream until soft peaks begin to form (do not overbeat). Add to gelatin mixture, blending completely (mixture will be runny). Pour into prepared pan, cover with plastic wrap and refrigerate several hours or overnight.

To unmold, tilt pan in circular motion to allow air to circulate in bottom of mold (cloth soaked in lukewarm water, wrung dry and placed around outside of pan will also help). Place serving plate over top and invert mold into plate. Return to refrigerator and chill.

For decoration: Whip 1 cup cream until stiff. Remove bavarian from refrigerator and frost top and sides with some of the cream. Spoon remaining cream into pastry bag fitted with ¼-inch tip. Pipe outlines of 6 ovals around outer edge of top and 1 in center (or pipe ovals in center to resemble flower). Chill.

Heat remaining ¼ cup cream with chocolate in small saucepan over very low heat until chocolate is melted. Remove from heat and stir in liqueur. Let cool 10 minutes. Remove bavarian from refrigerator and carefully spoon chocolate mixture into ovals. Chill well.

Peppermint Bavarian with Mint Fudge Sauce

8 servings

1 tablespoon unflavored gelatin
1 cup milk

3 egg yolks
½ cup sugar
1 tablespoon vanilla
1 teaspoon peppermint extract

1 cup whipping cream
4 egg whites, room temperature
Pinch of salt

Mint Fudge Sauce*
½ cup finely crushed peppermint candy

Sprinkle gelatin over milk in heavy 1-quart saucepan. Let stand until gelatin is absorbed. Place over high heat and cook until milk is scalded.

Meanwhile, whisk yolks and sugar until pale and thick. Blend in ¼ cup scalded milk. Whisk mixture back into milk. Stir over low heat with wooden spoon until mixture is thick enough to coat back of spoon or registers 180°F on candy thermometer; do not boil. Immediately pour into bowl set in larger ice-filled bowl. Blend in vanilla and peppermint extracts. Let cool until slightly thickened, stirring occasionally, about 15 minutes; do not allow to set.

Beat cream until soft peaks form. Beat whites and salt until soft peaks form. Fold whipped cream into custard. Gently fold ¼ of whites into custard mixture, then fold custard into whites.

Rinse inside of 6-cup kugelhopf mold with cold water. Shake out excess; do not dry. Pour custard mixture into mold. Cover and chill overnight.

Just before serving, lightly oil platter. Set mold in hot water for 5 seconds. Invert mold onto platter. Drizzle with some of fudge sauce. Sprinkle with some of peppermint candy. Pass remaining sauce and candy separately.

*Mint Fudge Sauce

Makes 1⅔ cups

3 ounces unsweetened chocolate
¼ cup (½ stick) unsalted butter
½ cup light corn syrup
½ cup sugar

½ cup water
Pinch of salt
1 teaspoon vanilla
⅛ teaspoon peppermint extract

Melt chocolate and butter with corn syrup in double boiler over gently simmering water; stir until smooth. Blend in sugar, water and salt and cook until sugar dissolves. Remove from heat. Stir in vanilla and peppermint extracts. Serve hot or at room temperature. (*Can be prepared 2 weeks ahead and refrigerated. Reheat gently in double boiler if desired.*)

Cheesecake Mousse with Raspberry-Cognac Sauce

8 servings

¾ cup water
½ cup sugar
1½ tablespoons kirsch
1½ tablespoons Cognac or brandy
2 teaspoons unflavored gelatin
4 ounces cream cheese, room temperature
4 ounces ricotta cheese, room temperature
6 eggs, separated, room temperature
1 cup whipping cream, whipped

Raspberry-Cognac Sauce
1 10-ounce package frozen raspberries
1 tablespoon kirsch
1 tablespoon Cognac or brandy

Oil eight 6-ounce custard cups. Combine water, sugar, kirsch, Cognac and gelatin in small saucepan and stir over medium heat until gelatin dissolves. Combine cream cheese, ricotta and yolks in processor and blend well. Transfer to medium saucepan and stir over low heat until mixture thickens, about 5 minutes. Blend in gelatin mixture. Set pan in ice water and stir until cooled. Beat whites in large bowl of electric mixer until stiff but not dry. Fold cooled yolk mixture into whites alternately with whipped cream. Pour into prepared cups. Refrigerate for at least 6 hours.

For sauce: Combine raspberries, kirsch and Cognac in processor and puree until smooth. Strain if desired. Refrigerate.

To serve, run tip of small knife around top edge of each cup. Briefly immerse custard cups in warm water. Invert onto individual plates and top each with some of sauce. Pass remaining sauce separately.

Chilled Pumpkin Mousse with Rum Sabayon

8 servings

1 envelope unflavored gelatin
1/2 cup dark rum
2 cups (one 1-pound can) unsweetened pumpkin
1 teaspoon cinnamon
1/2 teaspoon salt
1/4 teaspoon ground cloves

4 egg yolks
1/2 cup firmly packed brown sugar

1/2 cup sugar
1/4 cup (1/2 stick) unsalted butter

4 egg whites, room temperature
1/8 teaspoon cream of tartar
Pinch of salt
3/4 cup well-chilled whipping cream
Rum Sabayon*

Soften gelatin in rum in small dish; set aside. Combine pumpkin, cinnamon, salt and cloves in large bowl; set aside.

Beat egg yolks in medium bowl until foamy. Add sugars and continue beating until pale yellow. Melt butter in top of double boiler over warm water. When just melted, add yolk mixture and cook, stirring frequently, until thickened, about 5 to 10 minutes; *do not overcook or eggs will curdle.* Add gelatin and beat until smooth and shiny, about 1 minute. Blend into pumpkin mixture. Let cool to room temperature.

Beat egg whites in another large bowl until foamy. Add cream of tartar and salt and continue beating until stiff. Fold into pumpkin. Whip cream until stiff and fold into pumpkin. Spoon mousse into 8 wine glasses or other dessert dishes. Cover and chill 24 hours. Pass rum sabayon separately.

*Rum Sabayon

8 egg yolks
3/4 cup white rum

1/2 cup plus 2 tablespoons sugar

Combine all ingredients in 2-quart stainless steel mixing bowl and beat at high speed of electric mixer until light and syrupy. Place over pan of gently simmering water and continue beating until thick and frothy (if mixture thickens before becoming frothy, sauce will resemble custard rather than sabayon). Let cool to room temperature before serving.

❦ Mousses

Light and ethereal in texture, yet intensely rich in flavor, the dessert mousse is among the most sensually pleasing of all desserts. And to add to its charm, it is gorgeous to look at.

The mousse has a long and illustrious history beginning, according to some sources, in about 1066 when the Normans brought recipes for these delicacies with them on the conquest of Britain. But it was in the nineteenth century that chefs created the most elaborate and sumptuous versions—often using so much gelatin to create towering and ornate confections that they were much better to look at than to eat. Modern versions are simpler and more delectable, and use only enough gelatin to hold a soft shape.

As festive and dramatic as the mousse can be, it is not a prima donna like its demanding cousin the soufflé. A mousse can be made completely a day or two ahead and asks only minimal attention at the last minute. While creating the perfect mousse is not difficult, every step in its creation must be performed with care and precision.

The mousse's light and gossamer texture—a stabilized aerated base—can be created from many different basic ingredients. The flavor base may be chocolate, fruit puree, syrup, liqueur or nut praline—a wonderful array of choices. Chocolate and liquid flavorings are usually combined with egg yolks to make a custardy sauce. A smooth, long-lasting liaison is formed by whisking the melted chocolate or liquid and egg yolks in a heavy pan until they are even thicker than hollandaise and other emulsion sauces. The key is keeping the heat low enough and the whisking wrist speedy enough so the yolk mixture doesn't curdle.

The egg yolk base must be cool before whipped cream or beaten egg whites are folded in or it will collapse into a puddle. Both the cream and whites must be stiff enough to thicken the mousse. For maximum volume, the whites are warmed to room temperature and whipped until they peak, becoming stiff but not dry. Whipping cream, on the other hand, reaches maximum volume in a chilled bowl and when beaten with a chilled whisk.

For optimum flavor, refrigerate the mousse for several hours or overnight. It may be presented as is and unadorned, but because we like to gild the lily occasionally, we have included a number of finishing touches.

Walnut Cream Dessert

10 servings

4 egg yolks
¼ cup sugar
1 tablespoon all purpose flour
1 tablespoon arrowroot
¾ cup whipping cream
¾ cup milk
3 tablespoons kirsch

1 cup (2 sticks) butter, room temperature
¾ cup sugar
2 cups walnuts, toasted and finely chopped
Chocolate Sauce*

Line 8-inch soufflé dish with plastic wrap, letting excess extend over edge; set aside. Combine yolks, ¼ cup sugar, flour and arrowroot in medium saucepan. Whisk in cream, milk and kirsch. Place over medium heat and whisk constantly until mixture has thickened. Let stand until completely cooled.

Beat butter and ¾ cup sugar in medium bowl until light and fluffy. Fold in walnuts and cooled yolk mixture. Turn into mold. Cover and refrigerate 6 hours or overnight. Unmold and serve immediately with chocolate sauce.

*Chocolate Sauce

¼ cup (½ stick) butter	½ cup sugar
½ cup unsweetened cocoa powder	½ cup whipping cream

Melt butter in medium saucepan over medium heat. Reduce heat and whisk in cocoa and sugar. Gradually add cream, stirring constantly until mixture is smooth and heated through. Serve warm.

Honey Hazelnut Mousse with Apricot Sauce

4 servings

Hazelnut Praline
  ¼ cup hazelnuts

  ¼ cup sugar

Honey Mousse
  6 egg yolks, room temperature
  ½ cup honey
  1 cup whipping cream
  1 egg white, room temperature
    Pinch of salt
    Pinch of cream of tartar

Apricot Sauce
  3 ounces dried apricots (about
    ½ cup firmly packed)

  1½ cups water
  ⅓ cup sugar
    2 tablespoons apricot brandy or
      Cognac
      Apricot nectar

  4 nasturtiums or other fresh
    flowers (garnish)

  4 fresh apricots, poached
    (optional)*

For praline: Preheat oven to 350°F. Bake hazelnuts until brown, about 15 minutes. Rub in towel, over sieve or between hands to remove skins; set aside.

Butter baking sheet. Place sugar in small heavy saucepan. Pour in water to cover. Cook over low heat until sugar melts, shaking pan occasionally. Increase heat and cook until sugar caramelizes and is golden brown, washing down any crystals on sides of pan with brush dipped in cold water. Quickly stir in hazelnuts and pour out onto prepared sheet. *Immediately* remove 4 hazelnuts for garnish. Let remaining praline harden, then chop coarsely.

For mousse: Beat egg yolks and honey until thick and pale yellow and mixture forms a ribbon when dropped from beater. Pour into double boiler, set over gently simmering water and whisk several minutes until *very* thick. Return to mixing bowl and beat until cool.

Beat whipping cream in chilled bowl until stiff. Beat egg white until foamy. Add salt and cream of tartar and beat until stiff but not dry. Stir ¼ of whites into yolk mixture to loosen. Gently fold in remainder until almost incorporated, then fold in whipped cream. Fold in chopped praline. Cover and refrigerate several hours or overnight.

For apricot sauce: Combine apricots, water and sugar in heavy saucepan and cook over low heat until sugar is dissolved. Increase heat and simmer until apricots are very soft and liquid is reduced to thick syrup, about 25 minutes, stirring frequently during last 5 minutes to prevent burning. Wash off any sugar crystals on sides of pan with brush dipped in cold water. Transfer to processor or blender and puree; strain. Stir in brandy. Thin sauce with apricot nectar if necessary. Cover and refrigerate.

To serve, divide mousse among 4 goblets. Top with apricot sauce and place reserved hazelnut in center of each. Set goblets on serving plates and garnish plates with a fresh flower. Let mousse stand at room temperature for 15 minutes before serving.

*If using poached apricots, serve mousse on individual plates or in dessert bowls and garnish each with 2 apricot halves.

Chocolate Mousse Flowerpots

Present this dessert in ceramic cachepots topped with chocolate flowers; each flowerpot serves two. See page 29 for tips on preparing the Crème Anglaise.

10 servings

Crème Anglaise
3 cups milk
1 cup whipping cream
10 egg yolks, room temperature
1 cup sugar

Chocolate Mousse
¹/₂ cup sugar
¹/₂ cup water

4 egg whites, room temperature
¹/₄ teaspoon cream of tartar
2 cups whipping cream, whipped to soft peaks

1 cup unsweetened cocoa powder
4 ounces semisweet chocolate, melted and cooled
3 tablespoons instant espresso powder

Chocolate Flowers
10 ounces coating chocolate or milk chocolate, coarsely chopped
¹/₄ cup light corn syrup

For crème anglaise: Bring milk and cream to boil in heavy large saucepan. Meanwhile, beat yolks and sugar in large bowl of electric mixer until pale yellow and slowly dissolving ribbon forms when beaters are lifted. Slowly pour 1 cup of hot milk mixture onto yolks, beating constantly. Return mixture to saucepan and stir over medium-low heat until mixture thickens and leaves path on back of spoon when finger is drawn across; *do not boil*. Pour through fine strainer into large bowl set into bowl of ice water and cool to room temperature, stirring occasionally. Cover tightly and refrigerate for at least 2 hours.

For mousse: Heat sugar and water in heavy small saucepan over low heat, swirling pan occasionally, until sugar dissolves. Increase heat and boil until mixture registers 260°F (hard-ball stage) on candy thermometer.

Meanwhile, beat whites and cream of tartar in large bowl of electric mixer until soft peaks form. Slowly pour in hot syrup, beating until mixture is cool, about 5 minutes. Gently fold in whipped cream, cocoa powder, melted chocolate and espresso. Cover mousse and refrigerate 1 hour.

For flowers: Line jelly roll pan with waxed paper. Melt chocolate with corn syrup, stirring until mixture is smooth. Pour into prepared pan. Spread to thickness of ¹/₄ inch, using metal spatula. Let chocolate mixture cool to room temperature.

Transfer paper with chocolate to work surface. Place second sheet of waxed paper atop chocolate. Roll chocolate out to ¹/₈-inch thickness. Cut into twenty 1-inch rounds, using cookie cutter. Roll 1 round into tight funnel shape for flower center. Gather 3 more rounds around center, forming petals. Squeeze together at base. Place on waxed paper-lined plate. Repeat with remaining chocolate, forming 5 flowers. Refrigerate until flowers are firm.

To assemble: Divide crème anglaise among five 2-cup cachepots or other porcelain dishes shaped like flowerpots. Top with chocolate mousse, mounding slightly in center. Set chocolate flower atop each. Refrigerate until 20 minutes before serving. (*Can be prepared 2 days ahead.*)

Chocolate Mousse with Brandied Custard Sauce

An easy one-work-bowl preparation in the food processor.

12 servings

3/4 cup sugar
1/2 cup water
1 tablespoon white vinegar
1 tablespoon water

8 egg whites
4 ounces unsweetened chocolate, broken into pieces

4 ounces sweet chocolate, broken into pieces
2 teaspoons freeze-dried coffee
7 egg yolks
2 teaspoons vanilla
Brandied Custard Sauce*

Combine 1/4 cup sugar and 1/2 cup water in heavy 1-quart saucepan and bring to simmer over medium heat, swirling pan occasionally to dissolve sugar completely. Mix vinegar and 1 tablespoon water in cup.

Combine egg whites and 1/4 cup sugar in processor work bowl and blend 8 seconds. With machine running, pour vinegar mixture through feed tube and process until whites are whipped and hold their shape, about 3 minutes. Gently transfer to 1-quart mixing bowl. Combine chocolates, coffee and remaining 1/4 cup sugar in work bowl and chop using 6 on/off turns, then process until chocolate is as fine as sugar, about 1 minute, stopping as necessary to scrape down sides and cover of work bowl. With machine running, pour simmering sugar syrup through feed tube and blend until chocolate is melted, about 30 seconds. Scrape down work bowl. Add yolks and vanilla and mix using 3 on/off turns. Spoon whites onto chocolate mixture and blend using 2 on/off turns just until whites are incorporated. (Some streaks of egg white may remain; do not overprocess. Remove steel knife and blend mixture gently with spatula if necessary.) Run spatula around sides of work bowl to loosen mixture. Transfer to 6-cup soufflé dish or 12 individual 1/2-cup ramekins. Cover with plastic wrap. Chill at least 8 hours. Serve with brandied custard sauce.

Can be refrigerated several days or frozen.

*Brandied Custard Sauce

Makes about 1 3/4 cups

7 egg yolks
1/2 cup sugar
Pinch of salt

1 1/2 cups milk
2 tablespoons Cognac

Combine yolks, sugar and salt in processor work bowl and blend until thick and lemon colored, about 1 minute. With machine running, slowly pour 1 cup milk through feed tube. Transfer mixture to heavy medium saucepan. Blend in remaining 1/2 cup milk. Cook over low heat, stirring constantly, until sauce is thickened and lightly coats spoon, about 15 to 20 minutes (mixture should register 180°F on instant-reading thermometer); *do not boil.* Strain into metal bowl. Set in bowl of ice water to cool quickly, stirring several times. Blend in Cognac. Cool completely. Cover and refrigerate until ready to serve.

Three Chocolate Mousses with Orange Cream

A spectacular presentation: ovals of white, milk and dark chocolate served on a pool of orange custard sauce.

8 to 10 servings

Chocolate Mousses
(makes about 1 quart of each mousse)
6 ounces semisweet chocolate, coarsely chopped
4 ounces milk chocolate, coarsely chopped
4 ounces white chocolate, coarsely chopped
12 tablespoons (1½ sticks) unsalted butter, room temperature

9 eggs, separated, room temperature
1½ cups powdered sugar

¼ teaspoon cream of tartar
¼ teaspoon salt

3 cups whipping cream
2 teaspoons vanilla

Orange Cream (makes about 2 cups)
1¼ cups milk
½ cup sugar
4 egg yolks, room temperature
½ cup strained fresh orange juice, room temperature
1½ teaspoons cornstarch
1 tablespoon orange liqueur

Candied Orange Peel*
Melted semisweet chocolate

For mousses: Place each chocolate in individual large heatproof bowl. Set bowls into simmering water just until chocolate is melted, stirring occasionally. Remove from heat. Add 4 tablespoons butter to *each* bowl and stir until melted (mixture may separate).

Combine yolks and powdered sugar in large bowl of electric mixer and beat at high speed until mixture forms slowly dissolving ribbon when beaters are lifted, about 3 minutes. Place bowl in pan of simmering water (or transfer mixture to top of double boiler set over simmering water) and beat constantly with whisk or portable electric mixer until very thick (do not overheat or mixture will curdle). Immediately stir ⅓ of yolk mixture into each chocolate.

Combine whites, cream of tartar and salt in large bowl and beat until stiff but not dry. Gently fold about ½ cup of whites into each bowl of chocolate, then fold ⅓ of remaining whites into each chocolate mixture. Whip cream and vanilla in large bowl until soft peaks form. Fold ⅓ of cream into each bowl of chocolate. Cover mousses and chill until set, preferably overnight.

For orange cream: Bring milk to simmer in heavy large saucepan. Combine sugar and yolks in large bowl of electric mixer and beat at high speed until mixture forms slowly dissolving ribbon when beaters are lifted. Mix in orange juice and cornstarch. Beat in hot milk drop by drop. Return mixture to saucepan, place over medium heat and cook, stirring constantly, until mixture thickens and coats spoon, about 10 minutes; *do not boil or eggs will curdle.* Remove from heat and let cool. Stir in liqueur. Cover and refrigerate.

To serve, divide orange cream evenly among shallow dessert dishes. Top with small oval scoops of each mousse. Sprinkle mousse with candied orange peel and drizzle with melted semisweet chocolate (a fork works well for this).

*Candied Orange Peel

Makes about ½ cup

2 large oranges

6 tablespoons sugar

¼ cup water

Using vegetable peeler, remove colored part of peel from oranges in pieces as wide as possible. Cut into thin julienne, discarding ragged edges. Blanch peel in small saucepan of boiling water 5 minutes. Drain; pat dry.

Combine sugar and ¼ cup water in same saucepan and cook over low heat until sugar is melted, swirling pan occasionally. Stir in peel, increase heat to medium and cook until peel is glazed and candied, about 30 minutes. Remove from syrup using slotted spoon and arrange on rack to dry, separating pieces. Store in airtight container.

Chocolate Mousse with Chocolate Crust

The combination of light rum and Marsala gives this mousse very special flavor.

10 to 12 servings

Crust
- 1 8½-ounce package chocolate wafers, crushed
- 2 tablespoons (¼ stick) unsalted butter, melted
- 1½ tablespoons instant coffee powder
- 1½ tablespoons unsweetened cocoa powder

Mousse
- ⅓ cup Marsala
- 1 tablespoon unflavored gelatin
- 4 egg yolks

- ½ cup sugar
- ¾ cup light rum

- 12 ounces semisweet chocolate
- 1 tablespoon instant espresso powder
- ¼ cup (½ stick) unsalted butter, cut into small pieces
- 2 cups whipping cream, whipped

Chocolate leaves (optional garnish)

For crust: Combine crushed chocolate wafers, melted butter, coffee and cocoa powders in large bowl and mix well. Refrigerate half of mixture and press remainder evenly into bottom of 8-inch springform pan. Set aside.

For mousse: Combine Marsala and gelatin in small bowl and let stand until gelatin is softened. Combine yolks and sugar in top of double boiler and beat until thickened, about 2 to 3 minutes. Stir in rum. Set over simmering water and continue beating until mixture is hot and foamy. Remove from heat. Add gelatin mixture and stir until gelatin is thoroughly dissolved. Set pan in ice and beat just until cool, about 5 minutes.

Melt chocolate in top of double boiler set over simmering water. Add espresso powder and stir through. Remove from heat and beat in butter 1 piece at a time. Blend into egg mixture. Set in bowl of ice and continue beating until mixture is smooth and cool. Fold in whipped cream. Turn into prepared springform and refrigerate overnight.

Remove sides of springform pan. Pat remaining half of crumb mixture around sides and top edge of mousse (there will be extra crumbs). Decorate top of mousse with chocolate leaves if desired.

Dessert can be frozen up to 2 months. Flash freeze, then cover with plastic wrap and return to freezer.

Triple Chocolate Mousse in Grand Marnier Sauce

More like an elegant fudge than a mousse.

8 servings

1 cup water
1 cup sugar

¼ cup chopped walnuts
4 ounces semisweet chocolate, coarsely chopped
½ cup (1 stick) unsalted butter

¾ cup unsweetened cocoa powder
2 egg yolks, room temperature, beaten
2 egg whites, room temperature

Grand Marnier Sauce*

Bring water and sugar to boil in heavy small saucepan over low heat, swirling pan occasionally; do not stir. Let boil 1 minute. Cool sugar syrup completely.

Butter and sugar 2-cup loaf pan. Sprinkle walnuts in bottom. Melt chocolate and butter in top of double boiler set over gently simmering water. Stir in cocoa powder and ¼ cup sugar syrup (reserve remainder for another use). Remove from over water. Blend in yolks. Beat whites in medium bowl until stiff but not dry. Gently fold into chocolate mixture. Pour into prepared pan. Cover and refrigerate at least 2 hours.

To unmold, run very sharp knife along edges of mousse and invert onto platter. To serve, cut into 8 slices. Ladle some of sauce onto each plate and top with slice of mousse.

*Grand Marnier Sauce

Makes about 1½ cups

2 egg yolks
1 tablespoon sugar
1 cup milk, scalded

3 ounces vanilla ice cream
2 tablespoons Grand Marnier

Blend yolks and sugar in top of double boiler until creamy. Set over gently simmering water and whisk in milk in slow steady stream. Continue whisking until mixture is thick, about 12 minutes. Remove from over water. Stir in ice cream and liqueur. Transfer to small bowl. Refrigerate until ready to use.

Délice au Chocolat

Another cross between mousse and fudge, this dessert is perfumed with raspberry.

10 to 12 servings

12 ounces semisweet chocolate, coarsely chopped
¼ cup raspberry liqueur (preferably imported)
7 egg yolks, room temperature

2 cups (4 sticks) unsalted butter, cut into 32 pieces

Raspberry puree

Butter 3- to 4-cup decorative mold. Melt chocolate with liqueur in double boiler over gently simmering water. Whisk in yolks one at a time. Whisk in 28 pieces of butter two at a time. Remove from over water and whisk in remaining butter. Pour into prepared mold. Cover with foil and refrigerate at least 6 hours. (*Can be prepared 3 days ahead.*)

Just before serving, set mold into pan of hot water for 30 seconds. Run knife around edge of mold. Invert onto platter and cut into thin slices. Serve with raspberry puree.

Chocolate Bowl

This recipe will make up to six chocolate bowls. If fewer are desired, let extra chocolate harden, wrap tightly and store at room temperature.

Makes 6 bowls

Chocolate Bowl
  1 7-inch metal bowl

  2 pounds coating chocolate (preferably Semper brand), broken into 2-inch chunks

Sour Cream-Yogurt Filling
(makes enough for 2 bowls)
  1 envelope unflavored gelatin
  3 tablespoons frozen orange juice concentrate, thawed
  4 egg yolks
  ¾ cup plus 2 tablespoons sugar

  1 cup sour cream
  ½ cup plain lowfat yogurt
  3 tablespoons Grand Marnier
  1½ cups whipping cream
  2 tablespoons sugar

 14 thin orange slices
  1 cup apple jelly, mixed in blender 6 seconds (for glaze)
     Mint leaves and orange segments (optional garnish)

For chocolate bowl: Fill 7-inch metal bowl with water and freeze about 1 hour. Place large metal spoon in center of partially frozen mold so handle extends above rim. Freeze overnight.

Bring water to boil in large saucepan over medium-high heat. Remove from heat. Place chocolate in large stainless steel bowl and set over (not in) saucepan of hot water. Let chocolate melt, stirring occasionally. Set aside for 1 to 2 minutes to cool slightly.

Line baking sheet with parchment or waxed paper. Grip spoon handle and remove ice mold from bowl in one piece. Wipe mold with clean towel. Immediately dip ice mold into melted chocolate, covering sides completely. Invert over another bowl (to catch drips) and swirl mold to spread chocolate evenly around sides (do not swirl over saucepan or melted chocolate as water from mold will cause chocolate to bind). Hold mold until chocolate has set, about 30 seconds. Gently place mold on parchment or waxed paper and carefully release chocolate from mold with fingertip. Repeat for up to 6 bowls, wiping ice mold gently with towel between each dipping.

Remove any water that may have dripped into chocolate bowl by patting very gently with paper towels. Place another baking sheet in low oven briefly to warm slightly. When chocolate bowl is cool and hard, invert onto warmed baking sheet and rotate in circular motion to even rim of bowl, about 3 to 5 *seconds.* Transfer bowl to platter and refrigerate.

For filling: Combine gelatin and orange concentrate in small bowl and stir until gelatin is softened. Whisk egg yolks, sugar and gelatin mixture in top of double boiler set over simmering water until mixture falls from whisk in ribbons, about 3 to 5 minutes. Remove from heat and whisk until completely cool (mixture will become thick and stringy). Stir in sour cream and yogurt. Blend in Grand Marnier. Combine whipping cream and sugar in medium bowl and beat until soft peaks form. Gently fold into yogurt mixture.

Divide mixture evenly among chocolate bowls, filling almost to top. Chill just until top of filling is set. Arrange orange slices in decorative pattern over top. Carefully pour apple jelly glaze over, smoothing evenly. Refrigerate for several hours. Garnish with mint leaves and orange segments, if desired.

Chocolate Amaretto Terrine

16 servings

12 ounces semisweet chocolate

1½ cups sugar
½ cup water

1½ cups (3 sticks) unsalted butter, room temperature
2¾ cups unsweetened cocoa powder
3 egg yolks

2 eggs
¼ cup amaretto
2 teaspoons almond extract
2½ cups toasted slivered almonds

2 tablespoons unsweetened cocoa powder
2 cups whipping cream, whipped

Melt chocolate in top of double boiler over hot water. Cool to room temperature.

Combine sugar and water in heavy small saucepan and bring to boil over high heat. Cool syrup to room temperature.

Line bottom of 9 × 5-inch loaf pan with waxed paper. Lightly butter sides of pan. Beat butter and 2¾ cups cocoa in large bowl of electric mixer until smooth, scraping down sides of bowl frequently. Blend in yolks and eggs. Beat in cooled melted chocolate and syrup. Blend in amaretto and almond extract. Stir in 2 cups almonds. Spoon into prepared pan. Cover with plastic wrap and chill terrine overnight.

Run knife around sides of pan and invert terrine onto platter. Dust top with 2 tablespoons cocoa. Press remaining ½ cup almonds onto sides of terrine. Let stand 15 minutes. Cut into 16 slices. Top each slice with dollop of whipped cream and serve.

Chunky Chocolate Loaf

Great fun and sinfully rich, this is like a candy bar for grown-ups.

20 to 25 servings

2 ounces white chocolate

¾ cup whipping cream
2½ pounds semisweet chocolate, finely chopped
2 tablespoons Cognac

½ cup (1 stick) unsalted butter

2 cups mixed glacéed fruits or moist dried fruits
1 cup lightly toasted pecan halves
1 cup lightly toasted blanched almonds

Grease 12¾ × 4⅛ × 2½-inch loaf pan* and line bottom and sides with waxed paper. Melt white chocolate in double boiler over gently simmering water. Stir until smooth. Spoon or pipe design of white chocolate in bottom of pan. Refrigerate until chocolate is set.

Bring cream to boil in heavy medium saucepan. Remove from heat. Add ½ pound semisweet chocolate, cover and let stand 5 minutes. Stir until smooth. Cool. Blend in Cognac. Refrigerate until firm. Roll into about sixty ¾-inch truffles. Refrigerate.

Melt remaining 2 pounds semisweet chocolate and butter in double boiler over gently simmering water. Stir until smooth. Cool to room temperature. Mix ⅔ of chocolate mixture with fruit and nuts. Spread half of remaining chocolate mixture over white chocolate design and up sides of pan. Spoon in fruit and nut mixture, spreading evenly. Top with 4 rows of 15 truffles each. Cover with remaining chocolate mixture. Press down gently to eliminate any air pockets. Refrigerate until set. (*Can be prepared several days ahead.*)

Run hot sharp knife around edge of cake. Invert onto platter. Cut into very thin slices and serve.

*If unavailable, a 9-inch round cake pan can be used. Arrange truffles in single layer.

 *Soufflés*

Nancy's Grand Marnier Soufflé

6 servings

¼ cup (½ stick) butter
⅓ cup all purpose flour
⅛ teaspoon salt
1½ cups milk
4 egg yolks, beaten to blend
⅓ cup Grand Marnier

3 tablespoons sugar
1 tablespoon grated orange peel
½ teaspoon vanilla
6 egg whites
¼ teaspoon cream of tartar
Powdered sugar

Preheat oven to 375°F. Butter 2-quart soufflé dish. Melt butter in medium sauce-pan over low heat. Whisk in flour and salt. Increase heat to medium. Add milk and stir until smooth, thick and bubbly. Remove from heat. Add yolks, Grand Marnier, sugar, peel and vanilla. Using electric mixer, beat batter until thoroughly combined. Using clean dry beaters, beat whites with cream of tartar in large bowl to moderately stiff peaks. Gently fold whites into batter. Pour into prepared dish. Bake until soufflé is golden and tester inserted in center comes out clean, 30 to 35 minutes. Sprinkle with powdered sugar and serve immediately.

Orange Marmalade Soufflé

Topping this chilled soufflé with a generous spoonful of warm Grand Marnier sauce makes it particularly enticing.

6 to 8 servings

¼ cup Grand Marnier
1 tablespoon fresh lemon juice
1 tablespoon unflavored gelatin

5 eggs, separated
1 cup sugar
¾ cup fresh orange juice
⅓ cup orange marmalade
¼ teaspoon salt
½ teaspoon finely grated lemon peel

1 cup whipping cream

Garnish
½ cup whipping cream
2 teaspoons powdered sugar
½ cup mandarin orange segments, drained
Grand Marnier Sauce*

Prepare 1-quart soufflé dish with lightly oiled waxed paper collar extending 1 inch above rim of dish. Set aside.

Combine Grand Marnier and lemon juice in small bowl. Sprinkle gelatin over top and let stand until softened.

Combine egg yolks, ¾ cup sugar, orange juice, marmalade and salt in top of double boiler. Set over simmering water and cook, whisking constantly, until mixture thickens and coats spoon, about 5 minutes. Remove from heat. Stir in softened gelatin and grated lemon peel. Turn into large bowl. Let custard cool to room temperature.

Beat egg whites until foamy. Gradually add remaining ¼ cup sugar and continue beating until stiff peaks form. In another bowl, whip 1 cup cream until soft peaks form. Stir some of whites into cooled custard to lighten, then fold in remaining whites, blending well. Fold in whipped cream. Turn into prepared dish. Refrigerate until soufflé is firm and spongy.

For garnish: Whip remaining cream with powdered sugar until stiff. Spoon into pastry bag fitted with star tip. Pipe rosettes over top of soufflé. Decorate with orange segments. Serve with Grand Marnier sauce.

*Grand Marnier Sauce

2 cups milk
¼ cup (½ stick) butter
⅓ cup sugar

3 egg yolks, room temperature
⅓ cup sugar

2 tablespoons cornstarch
1 teaspoon vanilla
⅓ cup Grand Marnier
⅓ cup whipping cream

Combine milk, butter and ⅓ cup sugar in medium saucepan over medium heat and bring to boil, stirring occasionally.

Using electric mixer, beat yolks and remaining sugar in small bowl until thickened. Add cornstarch and continue beating until mixture is light and lemon colored. Gradually beat in enough hot milk to warm mixture slightly. Strain into remaining milk, whisking until blended. Place over medium heat and bring to boil. Remove from heat and stir in vanilla. Let stand until cool. Refrigerate until ready to serve. Just before serving, rewarm sauce over low heat, stirring in Grand Marnier and cream.

Hot Apricot Soufflé with Ginger-Nutmeg Sauce

Perfect partners: creamy soufflé and a zesty fresh ginger sauce.

6 servings

8 ounces dried apricots
¾ cup hot water

Ginger Sauce
½ cup water
1 1½ × 6-inch piece (about 3 ounces) fresh ginger, peeled and thinly sliced
6 tablespoons sugar

1½ cups half and half
1 whole nutmeg, roughly cracked

6 egg yolks, room temperature

1 teaspoon vanilla
Pinch of salt

Soufflé
½ cup sugar
4 eggs, separated, room temperature
¼ cup Apry or other apricot liqueur
1 tablespoon vanilla
Pinch of salt
Pinch of cream of tartar
Powdered sugar

Soak apricots in hot water overnight.

For sauce: Heat water, ginger and sugar in heavy small saucepan over low heat, swirling pan occasionally, until sugar dissolves. Increase heat and simmer until ginger is tender, about 20 minutes. Puree in blender. Pour through fine strainer into medium bowl, pressing on ginger with back of spoon.

Scald half and half in heavy medium saucepan. Add nutmeg. Let cool.

Reheat half and half to lukewarm. Remove from heat. Combine yolks, vanilla and salt in bowl. Slowly strain half and half into yolks, whisking constantly. Return to pan. Stir over medium heat until slightly thickened, about 5 minutes. Whisk until cool. Strain into ginger syrup. Cover and refrigerate. (*Can be prepared 1 day ahead.*)

For soufflé: Position rack on lowest shelf of oven and preheat to 400°F. Butter 7-cup soufflé dish and dust with sugar. Puree apricots with soaking liquid in blender until smooth. Measure ¾ cup plus 2 tablespoons puree into large bowl. Add ½ cup sugar, yolks, liqueur, vanilla and salt and beat with electric mixer until slowly dissolving ribbon forms when beaters are lifted. Beat whites and cream of tartar to soft peaks in another bowl. Fold ⅓ of whites into apricot mixture to lighten, then fold in remaining whites. Spoon into prepared dish. Bake until soufflé is puffed and light brown, about 20 minutes. Dust with powdered sugar and serve immediately, passing sauce separately.

Lebkuchen Soufflé with Dark Beer Sabayon

A rendition of a dessert served at Munich's three-star restaurant Aubergine.

6 to 8 servings

Lebkuchen Soufflé
- ¼ cup minced candied orange peel
- 3 tablespoons minced crystallized ginger
- 3 tablespoons dark rum

- ⅔ cup sugar
- ¼ cup all purpose flour
- 1 tablespoon grated lemon peel
- 1 teaspoon cinnamon
- ¼ teaspoon freshly grated nutmeg
- 2 cups half and half
- 4 egg yolks

- ⅓ cup finely chopped blanched almonds
- 6 egg whites, room temperature
- ¼ teaspoon salt
  Pinch of cream of tartar

Dark Beer Sabayon
- ¾ cup sugar
- ⅔ cup flat dark German beer
- 3 egg yolks
- 1 egg
- 1 tablespoon fresh lemon juice
- ½ teaspoon cinnamon

For soufflé: Combine orange peel and ginger in small bowl. Sprinkle with rum. Let stand until ready to use.

Combine sugar, flour, lemon peel, cinnamon and nutmeg in heavy medium saucepan. Whisk in half and half and yolks. Stir mixture over medium-low heat until thick and smooth, 8 to 10 minutes. Set in ice water, stirring frequently, until mixture is cold.

Position rack in center of oven and preheat to 400°F. Butter 2½-quart soufflé dish and dust with sugar. Fold rum mixture and almonds into yolk mixture. Beat whites, salt and cream of tartar until soft peaks form. Fold ¼ of whites into yolk mixture to loosen. Gently fold in remaining whites until no streaks of white remain. Pour into prepared baking dish. Bake soufflé until puffed and brown but not completely set, 30 to 35 minutes.

For sabayon: Ten minutes before soufflé is done, whisk all sabayon ingredients in top of large double boiler set over gently simmering water. Beat with portable electric mixer at low speed until mixture starts to thicken. Increase speed to medium and beat until sabayon is frothy and almost thick enough to form ribbon when beaters are lifted. Pour into heated sauceboat. Serve soufflé immediately. Pass dark beer sabayon separately.

Fig Soufflé with Parmesan

A delicious recipe that combines a cheese course and dessert in one.

6 servings

- 12 ounces dried figs
- ½ cup Marsala
- 1 tablespoon fennel seeds, lightly crushed

- 4 tablespoons sugar
- 2 tablespoons all purpose flour
- ¼ teaspoon salt
- ¾ cup milk or half and half
- 6 egg yolks, room temperature

- 7 egg whites, room temperature
  Pinch of cream of tartar

- ½ cup freshly grated Parmesan cheese
  Additional freshly grated Parmesan cheese (optional)
  Crème anglaise (see page 28) flavored with Marsala (optional)

Combine figs, Marsala and fennel seeds, cover and let stand at room temperature at least 24 hours or up to 1 week before using.

Cook figs and liquid in heavy large saucepan over medium-low heat until soft, stirring often, 45 to 60 minutes. Reserve 6 whole figs for garnish. Puree remaining figs in processor until smooth. Press puree through fine strainer.

Mix 3 tablespoons sugar, flour and salt in heavy medium saucepan. Add milk and bring to boil over medium-high heat, stirring constantly, until thick, about 1 minute. Beat in yolks one at a time. Whisk in fig puree.

Beat whites with cream of tartar in large bowl of electric mixer until stiff but not dry. Fold ¼ of whites into soufflé base to loosen, then fold in remainder.

Preheat oven to 400°F. Butter 1½-quart soufflé dish and sprinkle with remaining 1 tablespoon sugar. Spoon ⅓ of soufflé mixture into dish. Sprinkle with half of cheese, leaving ½-inch border. Repeat with another ⅓ of soufflé and remainder of cheese. Top to brim with remaining soufflé and smooth evenly with spatula. Run thumb around top ½ inch inside dish so soufflé will rise straight up. Bake until outside edges are cooked but inside is still soft and creamy, 15 to 20 minutes. Serve with reserved whole figs. Pass bowl of grated Parmesan or Marsala-flavored crème anglaise to accompany soufflé if desired.

Cointreau Soufflé in Puff Pastry

Pastry, sauce and soufflé base can be prepared ahead and dessert assembled and baked just before serving.

8 servings

Puff Pastry
2¾ cups all purpose flour
  1 cup cake flour
  2 cups (4 sticks) well-chilled unsalted butter, cut into ½-inch pieces
  1 cup (or more) water
  2 tablespoons fresh lemon juice
  1 teaspoon salt

  1 egg yolk blended with 1 teaspoon water

Raspberry Sauce
 10 ounces fresh or thawed and drained frozen raspberries
 ⅓ cup sifted powdered sugar (or to taste)

 ¼ cup red currant jelly
  2 tablespoons Cointreau

Cointreau Soufflé
  4 eggs, separated, room temperature
 ¾ cup milk
  5 tablespoons sugar
2½ tablespoons all purpose flour
    Pinch of salt
  1 small lemon
 ¼ cup Cointreau
    Pinch of cream of tartar

For pastry: Mix flours in large bowl; reserve ½ cup. Mix ½ cup butter into remaining flour with fingertips until mixture resembles coarse meal. Mix 1 cup water with lemon juice and salt. Blend into dough just until dough holds together, sprinkling 1 to 2 more tablespoons water over dough if necessary; do not overmix or pastry will be tough. Gather dough into ball and flatten into disc. Wrap in plastic; refrigerate 30 minutes.

Soften remaining 1½ cups butter by spreading across work surface using pastry scraper or palm. Work in reserved flour gradually until well blended. Form into ¾-inch disc.

Remove dough from refrigerator. Roll out on generously floured surface into circle about twice the diameter of butter disc. Arrange butter disc in center of dough circle. Fold sides of dough up over butter disc, meeting in center. Moisten dough with water if necessary and press edges together to seal and completely enclose butter.

Roll pastry out into ¾-inch-thick rectangle so 1 short end is parallel to work surface, rolling firmly and consistently without pounding or squeezing; avoid rolling over ends. (*If dough resists rolling or butter starts to soften and run, return dough to refrigerator until well chilled and firm.*) When rectangle is formed, roll dough in opposite direction at ends to flatten to same thickness as rest of dough. Brush off excess flour. Fold into thirds (as for business letter). Roll lightly over dough to even. Brush off excess flour. Repeat rolling and folding. Refrigerate pastry 1 hour.

Repeat rolling and folding 2 more times. Refrigerate pastry for 1 hour.

Repeat rolling and folding 2 more times. Cut pastry in half crosswise. Wrap each piece in plastic and refrigerate at least 2 hours, preferably overnight. (*Puff pastry can be prepared up to 2 days ahead and refrigerated or up to 6 months ahead and frozen.*)

Roll 1 piece of dough out into rectangle ⅛ inch thick (reserve remaining pastry for another use). Trim dough to 10 × 20-inch rectangle. Cut rectangle into eight 5-inch squares using ruler and very sharp knife. Transfer to baking sheet. Refrigerate 30 minutes.

Fold each pastry square in half diagonally to form a triangle. Starting at folded base of triangle ½ inch from right edge, cut ½-inch-wide strip to within 1 inch of triangle point (leave strip attached). Repeat on left side. Unfold triangle. Pick up point of right border strip and fold to left point inside cut border. Attach these points to each other with dab of water. Repeat with left border. Prick bottom of tartlet generously, using fork. Refrigerate tartlets at least 1 hour.

Set racks in upper and lower positions of oven and preheat to 425°F. Carefully brush top of pastry with egg mixture; do not allow egg to drip down sides or pastry will not rise. Bake tartlets on upper rack of oven until well puffed and top edges are golden brown, about 10 minutes. Prick centers of tartlets with fork. Reduce oven temperature to 350°F. Transfer tartlets to lower rack and continue baking until dry and crisp, about 15 to 20 minutes. Cool on wire rack until ready to prepare soufflé mixture.

For sauce: Press berries through fine sieve set over medium bowl to puree and remove seeds (or puree in processor, then strain). Stir in sugar, jelly and Cointreau. (*Sauce can be prepared 1 day ahead and refrigerated. Bring to room temperature before using.*)

For soufflé: Preheat oven to 400°F. Whisk 2 yolks in small bowl to blend. Whisk milk, 1 tablespoon sugar, flour and salt in heavy medium saucepan until smooth. Place mixture over low heat and whisk until very thick. Remove from heat. Stir heaping tablespoon milk mixture into yolks, then slowly whisk yolks back into milk mixture. Return to low heat and cook until bubbles appear. Remove from heat and grate peel of 1 small lemon directly into mixture. Squeeze lemon and stir 2 tablespoons juice into mixture. Blend in Cointreau. Whisk in remaining 2 yolks. (*Soufflé base can be prepared several hours ahead and set aside at room temperature; reheat before continuing.*) Beat egg whites with a pinch of cream of tartar in large bowl to soft peaks. Add remaining 4 tablespoons sugar 1 tablespoon at a time, beating until whites are stiff but not dry.

Return tartlet shells to oven 2 to 3 minutes to warm. Meanwhile, fold about ⅓ of whites into soufflé base to lighten. Gently fold in remaining whites in 2 batches. Spoon soufflé mixture into heated tartlet shells. Bake until soufflé is puffed and brown but still slightly soft in center, 10 to 15 minutes. Transfer tartlets to individual plates. Spoon sauce around tartlets and serve immediately.

Chocolate Omelet Soufflé with Cherry Preserves

This delicately flavored soufflé is baked in a shallow dish rather than the traditional deep mold.

4 servings

2 tablespoons (¼ stick) butter (for dish)
4 eggs, separated, room temperature
¼ cup sugar
¼ cup Dutch process cocoa powder

2 tablespoons orange liqueur (optional)
8 tablespoons cherry preserves
1 tablespoon powdered sugar

Position rack in upper third of oven and preheat to 375°F. Butter 9 × 14 × 2-inch glass oval gratin or baking dish.* Beat egg yolks in large bowl of electric mixer until pale yellow and slowly dissolving ribbon forms when beaters are lifted, about 8 minutes. Beat egg whites in another bowl until soft peaks form. Beat in sugar about 1 tablespoon at a time. Add cocoa to whites about 1 tablespoon at a time and continue beating until stiff but not dry. Gently fold yolks into egg white mixture, then fold in liqueur. Spoon cherry preserves into prepared dish in mounds, spacing evenly. Pour egg mixture over and smooth top with spatula. Bake until soufflé is puffy, about 15 minutes. Sprinkle with powdered sugar and serve immediately, including 2 portions of preserves with each serving.

*Soufflé can also be baked in metal or enamel gratin pan at 400°F.

Hot Brownie Soufflé with Vanilla Ice Cream Sauce

Tastes like a rich, moist brownie.

6 servings

½ cup (1 stick) butter, chopped
4 ounces unsweetened chocolate, coarsely chopped
1 cup sugar
4 egg yolks, room temperature
1 tablespoon instant coffee powder dissolved in 1 tablespoon rum or orange liqueur

1 teaspoon vanilla
¼ cup all purpose flour

5 egg whites, room temperature
Sugar
Vanilla Ice Cream Sauce*

Position rack in center of oven and preheat to 450°F. Butter 1-quart soufflé dish and sprinkle with sugar. Melt ½ cup butter with chocolate in heavy large saucepan over very low heat, stirring until smooth. Blend in ½ cup sugar, yolks, coffee mixture and vanilla. Stir in flour. (*Soufflé base can be prepared several hours ahead and set aside at cool room temperature. Reheat before continuing.*)

Beat whites in large bowl until soft peaks form. Gradually add remaining ½ cup sugar, beating constantly until whites are stiff but not dry. Fold ¼ of whites into chocolate, then fold chocolate back into remaining whites (be careful not to deflate mixture; a few streaks of white may remain). Turn batter into prepared dish. Sprinkle lightly with sugar. Bake 5 minutes. Reduce oven temperature to 400°F and continue baking until soufflé is puffed, about 20 minutes (center will remain moist). Serve immediately with sauce.

*Vanilla Ice Cream Sauce

Makes 2 cups

1 pint rich vanilla ice cream

2 tablespoons rum or orange liqueur

Place ice cream in medium bowl. Let soften at room temperature 10 minutes (or in refrigerator 30 minutes). Add rum and beat until smooth. Turn into small bowl and serve immediately.

2 ❦ Charlottes and Meringue Desserts

Though altogether diverse in flavor and appearance, the elegant, sophisticated desserts in this chapter have several essential features in common. For one thing, they are deceptively simple to prepare. All are chiefly or entirely do-ahead. And they are just the thing for those times when the *pièce de résistance* should be as light as a mousse or fresh fruit pudding, but as impressive as a towering *gâteau*.

Multiple components are what make these desserts so spectacular. Charlottes consist at the very least of an outer layer—typically génoise or ladyfingers—and a rich filling. But there are usually embellishments, too—among others, fruit puree, custard sauce and whipped cream rosettes. The same is true for the assortment of meringue confections: The meringue layers and at least one filling are the very minimum, but there are nearly always additional enhancements.

This is a season-spanning collection with recipes suitable for any festive occasion. When spring and summer berries are at their peak try Charlotte's Strawberry Charlotte (page 32), Broyage Torte with Strawberries (page 36), or Raspberry Délice (page 34). In the fall and winter months, Pumpkin Charlotte (page 31), Autumn Apple Meringue (page 33), and Mincemeat Torte with Bourbon Sauce (page 38) are refreshing new treatments for familiar ingredients. And such luscious creations as Bittersweet Chocolate Charlotte (page 28), meringue-layered Café Délice (page 37), and Market Place Marjolaine (page 42) will conclude a celebration dinner in grand style at any time of year.

🍎 Charlottes

Apple Charlotte

From Los Angeles pâtissier
Michel Richard.

8 to 10 servings

2 tablespoons (¼ stick) butter
2 large apples, peeled, seeded and
  cut into ¼-inch dice
2 tablespoons sugar

Apple Puree
⅓ cup whipping cream
1 teaspoon unflavored gelatin
2 large apples, peeled, seeded and
  cut into 1-inch chunks
1 cup apple juice
2 tablespoons fresh lemon juice
1½ tablespoons apple juice
1½ tablespoons cornstarch

Swiss Meringue
4 egg whites
¼ cup sugar

1 8-inch génoise (see page 101),
  cut into 3 layers (trim off very
  thin top brown crust and reserve
  for crumbs)
½ cup apple juice

Meringue Française
2 egg whites
¼ cup sugar

Sauce Normande
½ cup sugar
2 tablespoons water
1 teaspoon fresh lemon juice
½ cup whipping cream
⅓ cup apple cider

Melt butter in medium skillet over medium-high heat. Add apples and sugar and sauté, stirring gently but constantly, until apples are lightly browned and caramelized. Set aside.

For puree: Combine whipping cream and gelatin in small cup and let stand until gelatin is softened. Meanwhile, combine apples, 1 cup apple juice and lemon juice in blender and puree. Transfer to medium saucepan. Place over medium-high heat and bring to boil. Let boil gently 1 minute. Stir in softened gelatin and continue boiling gently 2 to 3 minutes. Combine 1½ tablespoons apple juice with cornstarch in another bowl and mix. Add to puree and cook 2 minutes.

For Swiss meringue: Combine egg whites and sugar in large bowl of electric mixer. Set bowl over (not in) simmering water and whisk gently until mixture is hot to touch. Immediately transfer bowl to electric mixer and beat at next to highest speed until bowl is cool. Quickly but thoroughly whisk/fold hot apple puree into meringue to form *chibouste*. Set chibouste aside.

Generously butter 8-inch springform pan. Line bottom and sides with large piece of plastic wrap. Set 1 layer of génoise, browned side down, in prepared pan. Brush generously with apple juice. Cover with 1-inch layer of chibouste. Sprinkle with sautéed apple. Top with second layer of génoise. Generously brush with apple juice. Spread with 1-inch layer of chibouste. Top with third layer of génoise, browned side up (be careful not to fill pan too full; cake layer should be even with top of pan). Cover with plastic wrap and refrigerate overnight.

For meringue Française: Beat egg whites in large bowl of electric mixer at medium speed until foamy. Gradually add sugar, beating constantly at next to highest speed until meringue is stiff and shiny, about 3 to 5 minutes.

Remove springform. Smooth top and sides of cake with spatula. Spoon meringue Française into pastry bag fitted with ½-inch plain tip. Starting at outer edge of cake, pipe meringue in petal (or large ladyfinger) shape toward center, tapering center ends and leaving 1½-inch circle in center. Pipe mound of meringue in center (top should now resemble daisy pattern).

Preheat broiler. Set charlotte on baking sheet and broil 6 to 7 inches from heat source until top is just lightly browned, *watching to prevent burning.*

Turn off oven. Break up reserved génoise crust and transfer to baking sheet. Let stand in oven to dry completely. Pour into plastic bag and crush with rolling pin. Gently press génoise crumbs around sides of charlotte. Transfer charlotte to serving platter. Refrigerate until ready to serve.

For sauce: Combine sugar, water and lemon juice in medium skillet and cook over high heat until mixture is medium dark brown, about 2 to 3 minutes. Remove from heat. Stir in cream and apple cider. Place over medium heat and cook until slightly thickened, about 3 to 5 minutes. Transfer to dish and serve with charlotte.

Chef Besson's Chilled Apple Charlotte with Raspberry Sauce (Charlotte Normande au Coulis de Framboises)

6 to 8 servings

20 to 25 ladyfingers

4 pounds Golden Delicious apples, peeled and rubbed with lemon
4 cups water
1¼ cups sugar
7½ tablespoons fresh lemon juice
1 teaspoon grated lemon peel
1 vanilla bean, split

Custard Filling
2 cups milk
1 vanilla bean, split
6 egg yolks, room temperature
¼ cup sugar

2 envelopes unflavored gelatin

½ cup water
1 cup whipping cream, beaten to soft peaks
3 tablespoons Calvados

Raspberry Sauce
2 cups fresh or thawed frozen raspberries
1 tablespoon kirsch
Powdered sugar

Chantilly Cream
1 cup whipping cream
1 tablespoon sugar
1 teaspoon vanilla

Candied violets

Line bottom and sides of 5-cup charlotte mold with ladyfingers rounded side out. Trim ladyfingers even with top; reserve trimmings.

Quarter 4 apples and remove cores. Cook water and sugar in large saucepan over low heat until sugar dissolves, swirling pan occasionally. Add 3 tablespoons lemon juice, peel and vanilla bean and bring to boil. Reduce heat and simmer 5 minutes. Add apple quarters and simmer until tender, about 10 minutes. Let cool in syrup.

Drain apples, reserving vanilla bean for another use. Finely dice half of poached apples. Drain in strainer. Thinly slice remaining poached apples.

Halve remaining uncooked apples and slice thinly. Transfer to heavy large skillet. Add remaining 4½ tablespoons lemon juice and cook over medium heat until tender and nearly all liquid has evaporated, stirring frequently, about 20 minutes. Puree in blender until smooth. Cool completely.

For filling: Bring milk and vanilla bean to boil in heavy large saucepan. Remove from heat and let stand 15 minutes. Remove vanilla bean and reserve for another use. Return milk to boil. Beat yolks and sugar in bowl until pale and thick. Gradually whisk in milk. Return mixture to saucepan and stir over low heat with wooden spoon until mixture is thick enough to coat back of spoon, about 10 minutes; do not boil or mixture will curdle.

Sprinkle gelatin over water in small bowl to soften. Set in pan of simmering water and stir until dissolved. Stir into hot custard. Mix in diced apples and apple puree. Set saucepan in large ice-filled bowl and stir until mixture starts to set. Immediately fold in whipped cream and Calvados. Spoon into prepared mold. Sprinkle with ladyfinger trimmings. Refrigerate until firm, at least 2 hours. (*Can be prepared 2 days ahead. Let stand at room temperature 1 hour before serving.*)

For sauce: Puree raspberries in blender with kirsch and powdered sugar to taste. Strain sauce and chill until ready to serve. (*Can be prepared 2 days ahead.*)

For chantilly cream: Beat cream, sugar and vanilla to soft peaks.

One hour before serving, unmold charlotte onto platter. Arrange poached apple slices in circle on top, overlapping slightly. Spoon chantilly cream into pastry bag fitted with medium star tip. Pipe rosettes decoratively along base and up sides of charlotte. Set violets on rosettes. To serve, spoon raspberry sauce onto plates. Cut charlotte into thin slices. Set slice on each plate. Garnish sauce with remaining poached apple slices.

Apple Charlotte with Apricot-Brandy Sauce

10 servings

Apple Filling
¼ cup (½ stick) butter
3 to 3½ pounds tart crisp apples, peeled, cored and cut into ¼-inch slices
2 to 3 tablespoons sugar
Finely grated peel of 1 medium lemon
Juice of ½ medium lemon
¼ cup apricot jam, strained

Apricot-Brandy Sauce
1 cup apricot jam
3 tablespoons water
1 tablespoon sugar
3 tablespoons brandy (or more to taste)

10 to 12 thin slices firm white bread, crusts trimmed
½ cup (1 stick) butter, clarified

For filling: Melt ¼ cup butter in large skillet over medium-high heat. Add apples and sauté until juice is rendered and comes to boil. Stir in sugar, lemon peel and lemon juice. Reduce heat to medium and cook until all liquid evaporates. If apples begin to lose shape and texture, remove from heat and drain remaining liquid from skillet. Stir in ¼ cup strained jam, blending well.

For sauce: Combine 1 cup apricot jam with water and sugar in small saucepan and bring to boil over medium-high heat, stirring occasionally. Let boil 2 to 3 minutes. Strain into small bowl. Let cool to lukewarm. Blend in brandy.

To assemble: Preheat oven to 400°F. Lightly butter 6-cup (No. 16) charlotte mold, 1½-quart soufflé dish or other deep, straight-sided 1½-quart baking dish. Cut 1 square and 4 semicircles of bread to fit bottom of mold. Heat several tablespoons clarified butter in large skillet. Add cut bread pieces and sauté until light golden. Set aside. Cut remaining bread slices in half lengthwise. Dip *1 side* of each piece into butter remaining in skillet, adding more clarified butter as necessary. Place sautéed bread pieces in bottom of mold. Line sides with remaining bread slices, buttered side out, overlapping slightly. Pack filling into mold. Tap mold on work surface to remove air pockets and distribute filling evenly. Trim excess bread above top rim of mold.

Bake charlotte 25 minutes. Press apples down in mold to repack. Continue baking until bread is lightly browned, about 10 to 15 minutes. Trim bread around top again if necessary. Let cool about 20 minutes. Invert charlotte onto rimmed large platter. Spoon half of sauce over top. Pour remaining sauce around base and serve immediately.

❦ Charlottes

The charlotte is a classic do-ahead dessert that is also a master of disguise. It can assume many shapes, be encased in just about anything from buttered bread to madeleines, have a variety of hot or cold fillings and be sauced and decorated in an infinite number of ways. Apparently the French—who invented it in the first place—had just as hard a time defining what a charlotte should be, because even today the name is shared by quite different desserts.

They are traditionally prepared in French charlotte molds, flared cylinders of tin-washed metal adorned with two heart-shaped handles. The sloping sides allow the dessert to slide out easily when inverted. However, charlottes can be assembled in almost any deep pan with slightly tapered sides. For instance, the cooling Coffee Parfait Charlottes use individual soufflé dishes, but bowls or timbale molds can be substituted. For straight-sided desserts, a springform or deep layer pan with removable bottom is ideal.

Among their glorious possibilities, charlottes can be wrapped in ladyfingers, sponge cake, eclairs, cookies, madeleines, jelly roll slices or bread. Delicate ladyfingers are typically used for chilled charlottes. The delectable Bittersweet Chocolate Charlotte, filled with a creamy mousse and served with a smooth crème anglaise, is an irresistible example of this version. The festive Pumpkin Charlotte adds a delightful twist: The ladyfingers are coated with gingersnap crumbs for added flavor and a pleasing bit of crunch. If you are pressed for time, you can purchase the ladyfingers, but they are best made from scratch—prepare them in large quantities and store in an airtight container for a few weeks, or in the freezer for several months. When brushed with dessert syrup or lightly dipped in liqueur, the ladyfingers will soften and expand slightly to fill any holes. But be careful: If moistened too much they will have a tendency to disintegrate.

Overlapping slices of buttered bread are characteristic of hot fruit charlottes such as the Apple Charlotte with Apricot-Brandy Sauce. Just remember that the fruit mixture must be thick and dry; otherwise it will soften the lining and the dessert will collapse.

Tips and Techniques

- Before substituting another mold, determine how much it holds by measuring its capacity with water.
- Use tin-washed charlotte molds or ceramic molds for charlottes that are baked. Aluminum charlotte molds are good only for chilled types.
- For easy unmolding of chilled charlottes, first line the mold with waxed or parchment paper, especially if it is deep and the filling is delicate.
- To turn out a charlotte from an unlined pan, dip the mold in warm water to the depth of its contents. Place a serving plate over the top and, holding tightly, invert the plate and mold. Shake them gently and remove the mold carefully. Repeat the process if necessary. Or, place the platter over the mold and, holding tightly, invert. Soak a kitchen towel in hot water, wring dry and press all around the pan. Shake mold gently and remove. If the charlotte does not slide out easily, reapply the hot, damp towel until it does.

Chocolate Charlottes

8 to 10 servings

32 to 40 crisp ladyfingers (preferably French)*

12 ounces semisweet chocolate
3/4 cup water
1/2 cup sugar
1 vanilla bean, split

6 egg yolks

3 cups whipping cream

Vanilla custard sauce (use your favorite recipe or see *Crème Anglaise* below)

Line bottom of individual charlotte molds with waxed paper. Arrange 4 ladyfingers on sides of each mold, trimming ends to make them even with top of mold.

Slowly melt chocolate; stir until smooth, then set aside. Combine water and sugar in small saucepan and heat to boiling, shaking pan gently until sugar is dissolved. Let cool slightly, then add vanilla bean and steep about 10 minutes.

Put yolks into top of double boiler and set over simmering water. Remove vanilla bean from syrup. Slowly add syrup to yolks and beat with whisk using back-and-forth motion until yolks have thickened, about 5 minutes. Transfer to blender or processor and whip until cool. Turn into large bowl and whisk in melted chocolate.

Whip cream until stiff and fold into yolk mixture until well combined. Pour into prepared charlotte molds and chill.

To serve, unmold on dessert plates and carefully remove waxed paper. Pass chilled custard sauce separately.

*If using softer ladyfingers, toast in 200°F to 250°F oven until crisp.

Bittersweet Chocolate Charlotte

This recipe is one of the signature desserts of the late Jean Bertranou of L'Ermitage in Los Angeles.

8 to 10 servings

Chocolate Mousse
2 1/2 cups whipping cream
2/3 cup water
1/4 cup plus 2 tablespoons sugar
6 egg yolks, lightly beaten
8 ounces semisweet or bittersweet chocolate, melted and cooled

Crème Anglaise
2 cups milk

1 vanilla bean, split lengthwise, or 1/2 teaspoon vanilla extract
4 egg yolks
1/2 cup sugar

12 to 18 ladyfingers

Chocolate curls or large chocolate roll (garnish)

For mousse: Whip cream until stiff. Refrigerate until ready to use. Combine water and sugar in top of large double boiler set over hot water and stir until sugar is dissolved. Gradually add yolks, whisking constantly until mixture forms medium-stiff peaks, about 10 minutes (do not stop whisking or mixture will fall). Transfer to large bowl and mix until bottom of bowl is cool. Beat in chocolate. Stir in small amount of cream to lighten. Gently fold in remaining whipped cream.

For crème anglaise: Combine milk and vanilla bean in 2-quart saucepan and bring mixture to boil. Remove from heat and let stand for 10 minutes. Remove vanilla bean. Strain milk through 2 layers of moistened cheesecloth. Combine yolks and sugar in large bowl of electric mixer and beat until mixture is pale yellow and forms slowly dissolving ribbon when beaters are lifted. Gradually beat in milk. Pour mixture back into saucepan. Place over medium heat and cook until thickened, stirring constantly, about 3 minutes; do not boil or mixture will curdle. Cool to room temperature, stirring occasionally. Chill until ready to use.

🍎 Crème Anglaise

Custard sauce or "crème anglaise," the most useful of the French dessert sauces, is made from only four ingredients—milk, egg yolks, sugar and flavoring. The sauce is the basis of many classic desserts, including bavarian cream, charlottes and ice cream.

Custard sauce is quick to prepare but requires close attention. The sauce thickens only slightly, from the gradual heating of the egg yolks. If exposed to too high heat, if cooked too long or if not stirred continuously, the yolks will coagulate like scrambled eggs.

Organization is very important. Ready all utensils—whisk, wooden spoon, strainer and mixing bowl—before beginning the recipe.

Split vanilla bean near one end and continue almost to the other, so ends are still joined. Bean can be rinsed, dried and reused several times. A teaspoon of pure vanilla extract can be substituted for the bean; add the extract to the finished, cooled sauce.

To make stirring easier and to help prevent mixture from sticking to sides of pan, use a heavy-bottomed enameled or stainless steel saucepan with a rounded rather than straight bottom. Be sure to reach entire bottom surface of saucepan when stirring.

If sauce curdles and looks lumpy, gradually pour it into a blender or food processor with the machine running. This will save the sauce (unless it is very badly curdled), but will make the texture frothy rather than velvety. To remedy this, let it stand in a bowl for one hour, stirring occasionally.

To assemble: Lightly butter 8-cup (No. 18) charlotte mold. Line bottom with waxed paper. Trim 1 rounded end of each ladyfinger to square off. Spoon mousse into large pastry bag fitted with large tip. Pipe layer about 1 inch deep over bottom of mold. Line sides of mold with ladyfingers, trimmed end up and rounded side out. Pipe remaining mousse into mold. Tap mold very lightly on work surface to remove any air pockets and distribute mousse evenly. Refrigerate until completely set.

To serve, invert charlotte onto rimmed large plate. Peel off waxed paper. Pour crème anglaise around base. Garnish top center with chocolate curls.

Coffee Parfait Charlottes

10 servings

Coffee Parfait
1⅓ cups water
1 cup sugar
2 tablespoons dark rum
6 egg yolks
2 tablespoons instant espresso powder dissolved in 2 tablespoons boiling water

¾ cup whipping cream
30 3½-inch ladyfingers
½ cup whipping cream
1 tablespoon sugar
2 teaspoons coffee liqueur
10 candy coffee beans

For parfait: Combine water and sugar in small saucepan and bring to boil over high heat, stirring constantly to dissolve sugar. Transfer ⅔ cup hot syrup to small bowl. Blend in rum and set aside. Combine yolks in large bowl of electric mixer and set over pan of hot water. Pour ⅔ cup of remaining hot syrup over yolks in thin steady stream, whisking constantly until mixture holds peaks, about 5 minutes. Transfer bowl to mixer and beat on medium speed until bottom of bowl is cool. Stir in 1 tablespoon dissolved espresso. Taste and add more espresso as desired. Whip cream in another bowl until stiff. Gently fold cream into coffee mixture, blending well.

Lightly butter ten ⅔-cup ceramic soufflé dishes. Line bottoms of dishes with waxed paper. Cut 2 ladyfingers into ten ¾-inch pieces. Saturate pieces with reserved rum syrup. Cut remaining ladyfingers in half crosswise and brush lightly with rum syrup. Line sides of molds with halved ladyfingers, cut end up and rounded side out. Fill molds half full with coffee parfait. Set ¾-inch piece of ladyfinger in center of each. Top with remaining parfait. Gently tap molds on counter to distribute parfait evenly. Freeze until completely set, then cover with plastic wrap until ready to use.

To serve, dip dishes in hot water several seconds to loosen charlottes. Invert onto individual dessert plates. Peel off waxed paper. Whip remaining ½ cup cream with sugar and liqueur until stiff. Spoon into small pastry bag fitted with star tip. Pipe whipped cream rosette in center of each charlotte. Top with candy coffee bean. Serve immediately.

Pear Charlotte with Raspberry Sauce

8 servings

20 ladyfingers (about), separated

Pear Filling
¾ cup whipping cream
1⅓ cups milk
½ vanilla bean, split
4 egg yolks
⅓ cup sugar

1 envelope unflavored gelatin
2½ tablespoons cold water

2 ripe pears
Juice of 1 lemon

Raspberry Sauce
2 1-pint baskets fresh raspberries

or one 10-ounce package frozen raspberries, thawed and drained
⅓ cup sugar or to taste
1 teaspoon fresh lemon juice or to taste

½ cup strained apricot jam
1 ripe pear
Fresh lemon juice
Almond Paste Leaves* and Chocolate Stem**
(optional garnishes)

Line bottom of 6-cup (No. 16) charlotte mold with waxed paper; lightly butter sides of mold. Trim ends of ladyfingers to a point and arrange in daisy pattern in bottom of mold rounded side down and pointed side in. Cut small circle from 1 ladyfinger and set in center of daisy. Cut ½ inch from ends of remaining ladyfingers and arrange against sides of mold trimmed ends down and rounded sides out. Set aside.

For filling: Whip cream in medium bowl until stiff. Cover and refrigerate. Combine milk and vanilla bean in medium saucepan and bring to boil over medium-high heat. Remove from heat. Let stand 5 minutes; discard vanilla bean. Whisk yolks and sugar in medium bowl until mixture is light and fluffy and falls from whisk in ribbons. Gradually whisk in milk. Transfer to saucepan. Cook over medium heat until thickened (thermometer should register 180°F), stirring constantly. Set saucepan in bowl of ice water. Let custard cool 5 minutes.

Meanwhile, combine gelatin and 2½ tablespoons cold water in small bowl. Set bowl in pan of hot water and stir to dissolve gelatin. Mix into custard. Return saucepan to ice water, whisking custard occasionally until thick and cool. Gently fold in whipped cream.

Peel, core and thinly slice 2 pears. Rub with lemon juice to prevent discoloration. Pour vanilla cream into mold to depth of 1 inch. Arrange single layer of pears over cream. Repeat layering twice, ending with layer of cream. (You should have 3 layers of pears and 4 layers of cream.) Cover with plastic; chill several hours or overnight.

For sauce: Puree raspberries in processor or blender. Strain to remove seeds. Transfer puree to medium bowl. Blend in sugar and fresh lemon juice.

Heat apricot jam in small saucepan. Pour ½ cup raspberry sauce onto serving platter with slightly raised edge. Run thin sharp knife around inside of mold, dip bottom briefly in hot water and invert charlotte into center of platter. Brush top with apricot jam to glaze. Spoon glaze over sides. Peel, core and halve pear; rub with lemon juice. Arrange pear half on top of charlotte cut side down. Brush with apricot jam. Place 2 almond paste leaves at top of pear and set chocolate stem in center. Refrigerate until ready to serve.

*Almond Paste Leaves
___

2 ounces almond paste   Powdered sugar
Green food coloring

Combine almond paste and drop of food coloring in small bowl and blend well, adding more food coloring if deeper shade of green is desired. Sprinkle work surface with powdered sugar. Roll mixture out thinly. Cut out 2 leaves. Score leaves with tip of small sharp knife to resemble veins.

**Chocolate Stem
___

½ ounce semisweet chocolate,
melted

Spoon or pipe short length of chocolate onto waxed paper. Refrigerate until hardened. Gently peel off paper.

Pumpkin Charlotte
___

10 to 12 servings

Gingersnap Crust
18 to 24 ladyfingers
⅓ cup sugar
¼ cup plus 2 tablespoons water
2 to 3 tablespoons dark rum
½ cup fine gingersnap crumbs

Pumpkin Filling
1 cup milk
½ cup firmly packed brown sugar
4 egg yolks
2 envelopes unflavored gelatin
1 1-pound can unsweetened pumpkin
2 teaspoons finely grated orange peel

¾ teaspoon pumpkin pie spice
1 cup whipping cream
⅓ cup sugar
4 egg whites

Spiced Almonds
¼ cup blanched slivered almonds (1 ounce)
1 tablespoon sugar
¼ teaspoon pumpkin pie spice

½ cup whipping cream
4½ teaspoons dark rum
1 tablespoon powdered sugar

For crust: Lightly butter bottom and sides of 9 × 3-inch springform pan. Trim 1 rounded end of ladyfingers to square off. Combine sugar and water in small saucepan and bring to boil over high heat, stirring constantly to dissolve sugar. Let cool. Blend in rum. Brush both sides of ladyfingers with syrup. Roll in gingersnap crumbs to coat. Line sides of springform with ladyfingers, cut end down and rounded side out.

For filling: Combine milk, brown sugar, yolks and gelatin in 2-quart saucepan over low heat and cook until thickened, stirring constantly. Remove from heat. Stir in pumpkin, orange peel and pumpkin pie spice, blending well. Whip cream with sugar in large bowl to soft peaks. Whip egg whites in another large bowl until stiff but not dry. Fold in pumpkin mixture, then whipped cream. Pour into springform, smoothing top. Refrigerate at least 6 hours.

For almonds: Generously grease baking sheet. Combine almonds, sugar and pumpkin pie spice in small skillet over low heat and cook until sugar melts and coats almonds, stirring occasionally. Turn almonds out onto prepared sheet. Let cool; separate pieces.

To serve, whip ½ cup cream to soft peaks. Add rum and powdered sugar and whip until stiff peaks form. Spoon cream into pastry bag fitted with decorative tip. Remove sides of springform. Transfer charlotte to serving platter. Pipe rosettes of cream over top, covering completely. Top with almonds.

Charlotte's Strawberry Charlotte

12 servings

Sponge Cake
- 4 egg yolks
- ¾ cup sugar
- 1 teaspoon vanilla
- ¾ cup sifted cake flour
- ¾ teaspoon baking powder
- ½ teaspoon salt
- 4 egg whites, room temperature
- Powdered sugar

Syrup
- ⅓ cup sugar
- ¼ cup plus 2 tablespoons water
- 2 to 3 tablespoons orange liqueur

Almond Cream
- 1 cup (2 sticks) unsalted butter, room temperature
- 1 cup superfine sugar
- ⅓ to ½ cup orange liqueur
- ¼ teaspoon almond extract
- 1⅓ cups lightly toasted ground almonds
- 2 cups whipping cream

- 4 cups fresh strawberries, hulled
- 1 cup whipped cream

For cake: Preheat oven to 375°F. Line 10 × 15-inch jelly roll pan with parchment or waxed paper; grease paper. Beat yolks in large bowl until light. Gradually add sugar, beating until creamy. Blend in vanilla. Resift cake flour with baking powder and salt. Gradually add flour mixture to yolk mixture, beating until smooth. Whip egg whites in another large bowl until stiff but not dry. Fold whites into batter. Pour batter into prepared pan, spreading evenly. Bake until tester inserted in center comes out clean, about 12 minutes. Lightly sprinkle powdered sugar over kitchen towel large enough to cover cake. Arrange towel sugared side down over cake. Holding towel taut at ends of pan, invert cake onto towel. Immediately peel off paper. Trim any rough edges. Roll cake up lengthwise in towel. Cool on wire rack.

For syrup: Combine sugar and water in small saucepan and bring to boil over high heat, stirring constantly to dissolve sugar. Let cool. Blend in liqueur.

For almond cream: Cream butter with sugar in large bowl until pale and fluffy. Beat in orange liqueur and almond extract. Mix in nuts. Whip cream lightly; fold into butter mixture.

To assemble: Line bottom of 9 × 3-inch springform pan or 2-quart soufflé dish with waxed paper. Lightly butter sides of pan. Unroll sponge cake and cut into long pieces to fit sides of pan; set aside remaining cake. Brush 1 side of cake pieces with syrup. Line sides of pan with cake, syrup side in. Spoon ⅓ of almond cream into pan. Set aside 16 uniform strawberries for garnish. Arrange layer of remaining strawberries stem end down over cream. Repeat layering, ending with cream. Trim excess cake at top. Arrange reserved cake over top (this will be bottom of finished charlotte), covering completely. Cover with waxed paper. Set plate on top and weight with heavy object (large can works well). Refrigerate charlotte for at least 8 hours.

To serve, invert charlotte onto serving platter. Peel off waxed paper. Brush reserved strawberries with syrup. Arrange around rim of charlotte. Spoon whipped cream into pastry bag fitted with star tip. Pipe stars around base of charlotte and between strawberries.

🍎 *Meringues*

Autumn Apple Meringue

6 servings

¼ cup raisins
¼ cup rum

Caramel
⅔ cup sugar
⅓ cup water
⅛ teaspoon cream of tartar

Apple Meringue
5 tart medium cooking apples, preferably Pippin or Greening (about 1¼ pounds)
½ lemon
2 tablespoons (¼ stick) unsalted butter
½ cup water

1 cup egg whites (about 8), room temperature
⅛ teaspoon salt
⅛ teaspoon cream of tartar
1 cup (16 tablespoons) sugar
⅓ cup walnuts, toasted and chopped

Apple Rum Cream Sauce
3 egg yolks, room temperature
⅓ cup sugar
1 cup whipping cream
1 teaspoon vanilla

Combine raisins and rum; set aside.

For caramel: Lightly grease wire rack and baking sheet. Combine sugar, water and cream of tartar in 2-quart charlotte or other mold. (If using porcelain mold that cannot be placed over direct heat, combine ingredients in saucepan.) Place over low heat and swirl mold occasionally until sugar is dissolved. Increase heat and continue cooking until sugar caramelizes, washing down any crystals clinging to sides of pan using brush dipped in cold water, about 10 minutes. Remove from heat and quickly tilt mold until caramel covers bottom and sides. Invert on rack set over baking sheet and let stand 5 minutes.

For apple meringue: Preheat oven to 350°F. Butter baking pan. Peel apples and rub with cut lemon. Quarter and core apples; chop coarsely into ⅓-inch pieces. Spread in buttered pan and dot with 2 tablespoons butter. Cover and bake, stirring occasionally, until apples are tender when pierced with knife, about 15 minutes. Drain through sieve set over bowl. Return ¾ cup apples with drained juices to pan (let remaining apples cool completely). Add water to pan, cover and bake until apples are soft enough to mash. Set aside for sauce.

Drain raisins, reserving rum, and pat dry with paper towels. Beat egg whites until foamy. Add salt and cream of tartar and continue beating until soft peaks form. Add sugar 1 tablespoon at a time and continue beating until meringue is stiff and glossy. Fold in raisins, walnuts and apple pieces. Turn into caramelized mold, smoothing top. Tap mold on counter and set in deep baking pan. Fill pan with enough simmering water to come ¾ up sides of mold. Bake until meringue is browned and has begun to shrink from sides of mold, 40 to 45 minutes. Let cool to room temperature, then refrigerate at least 3 hours.

For sauce: Beat egg yolks with sugar in medium bowl until lemon colored and mixture forms slowly dissolving ribbon when beaters are lifted. Combine apples for sauce and reserved rum in processor or blender and mix until smooth. Transfer to heavy large saucepan and add cream. Bring to simmer, then gradually stir into yolk mixture. Return to saucepan over low heat and stir with wooden spoon until mixture thickens and finger leaves a path when drawn across spoon; *do not boil or yolks will curdle.* Remove from heat and stir in vanilla. Place piece of plastic wrap on surface of sauce. Let cool, then chill thoroughly.

To serve, unmold meringue onto serving platter and surround with sauce.

Raspberry Délice

Makes 9

Meringues
1½ cups powdered sugar
3 ounces unblanched almonds, ground
4 egg whites, room temperature
¼ teaspoon cream of tartar
⅛ teaspoon salt

Raspberry Buttercream
6 egg yolks, room temperature
6 tablespoons sugar
1 cup (2 sticks) well-chilled unsalted butter, cubed
¼ cup Raspberry Sauce*

Grand Marnier Custard Sauce
3 egg yolks, room temperature
¼ cup sugar
1¼ cups milk, scalded
2 tablespoons Grand Marnier

Chocolate Spread
3 ounces semisweet chocolate, coarsely chopped
½ ounce unsweetened chocolate, coarsely chopped
3 tablespoons whipping cream

Fresh raspberries

For meringues: Preheat oven to 225°F. Line 2 baking sheets with parchment paper. Draw nine 3-inch circles on each sheet. Combine ¾ cup powdered sugar and almonds. Using electric mixer, beat whites with cream of tartar and salt until soft peaks form. Gradually add remaining powdered sugar and beat until stiff and shiny. Gently fold in almond mixture. Spoon meringue into pastry bag fitted with plain tip. Starting at center of circle, pipe meringue in spiral pattern, covering completely. Bake 1½ hours. Turn oven off. Leave meringues in oven with door ajar until completely dry. Remove from parchment paper. (*Can be prepared 1 day ahead. Store in airtight container in cool dry place.*)

For buttercream: Place yolks and sugar in processor. With machine running, add butter through feed tube and mix until smooth. Blend in raspberry sauce. Turn buttercream into bowl. Cover and refrigerate until ready to use. (*Can be prepared 1 day ahead.*)

For custard sauce: Beat yolks and sugar in heavy medium saucepan until slowly dissolving ribbon forms when beaters are lifted. Gradually whisk in milk. Place over medium-low heat and stir until sauce thickens enough to coat spoon and registers 180°F on candy thermometer. Set saucepan in ice-filled bowl. Stir sauce until cool. Blend in Grand Marnier. Strain if necessary to remove lumps. Cover and refrigerate. (*Can be prepared 1 day ahead.*)

For spread: Melt chocolates in double boiler over gently simmering water. Add cream and stir until smooth. Immediately spread flat surface of each meringue with thin layer of chocolate.

To assemble: Spoon buttercream into pastry bag fitted with star tip. Pipe rosettes around edge of chocolate spread to form buttercream ring. Arrange several raspberries inside buttercream. Stack 2 completed meringues together, berry sides up. Repeat to form 9 délices. Cover and refrigerate 24 hours.

To serve, spoon Grand Marnier sauce onto each plate. Top with délice. Pass remaining raspberry sauce separately if desired.

*Raspberry Sauce

Makes ³/₄ cup

6 ounces fresh raspberries	1 tablespoon raspberry liqueur
¼ cup sugar	1 teaspoon fresh lemon juice

Puree raspberries in processor. Blend in sugar, liqueur and lemon juice. Strain sauce through fine sieve to eliminate seeds. Refrigerate until ready to use. (*Can be prepared 2 days ahead.*)

Meringue with Vanilla Cream and Raspberry Sauce

A spectacular dessert. The meringue shell can be made several days ahead and filled just before serving.

6 to 8 servings

Meringue Shell
8 extra-large egg whites, room temperature (1¹/₃ cups)
2½ teaspoons vanilla
½ teaspoon cream of tartar
½ teaspoon salt
2½ cups sugar

Vanilla Cream
1 tablespoon unflavored gelatin
1 cup milk
1 cup sugar
1 extra-large egg, room temperature

2 cups whipping cream, well chilled
1 teaspoon vanilla

Caramel
1 cup sugar
½ cup water

Raspberries and peaches
Raspberry Sauce*

For meringue: Preheat oven to 200°F.

Line 2 baking sheets with parchment. Draw 11-inch circle on each, using 11-inch tart pan as guide. Beat 4 whites in large bowl until foamy. Add 1¼ teaspoons vanilla, ¼ teaspoon cream of tartar and ¼ teaspoon salt and beat until soft peaks form. Add ¾ cup sugar 1 tablespoon at a time, beating until stiff. Fold in ½ cup sugar.

Spoon meringue into pastry bag fitted with ½-inch plain tip. Pipe meringue completely over 1 circle on prepared sheet, beginning in center and spiraling outward to edge. Replace tip with ¾-inch (No. 9) plain tip. Pipe meringue on second sheet in ring around inner edge of circle. Pipe a second ring atop first. Bake until meringues are firm and dry but not colored, about 2½ hours. Cool to room temperature.

Preheat oven to 200°F. Make another batch of meringue as above, using remaining meringue ingredients. Spoon into pastry bag fitted with medium star tip (No. 4). Pipe dots of meringue around top edge of baked solid meringue circle. Top with baked ring to form shell. Pipe rosettes of meringue around rim of double ring and in rows on sides of shell, covering completely. Bake until dry, about 2½ hours. Cool completely. (*Can be prepared 2 days ahead. Store airtight.*)

For cream: Sprinkle gelatin onto ¼ cup milk in small cup. Whisk remaining ¾ cup milk, sugar and egg in heavy 2-quart saucepan to blend. Stir over medium heat until mixture coats back of wooden spoon and registers 180°F on candy thermometer. Remove from heat and add gelatin, stirring until dissolved. Transfer to bowl. Set into large bowl of ice water. Let mixture cool until gelatin just begins to set around edges, stirring frequently.

Transfer meringue shell to platter. Beat cream and vanilla until firm peaks form. Fold into gelatin mixture. Chill until beginning to hold shape, if necessary. Spoon into meringue shell, reserving ¼ of mixture for garnish if desired. Spoon reserved cream into pastry bag fitted with small star tip. Pipe decoratively atop cream in shell. Refrigerate up to 3 hours.

For caramel: Heat sugar and water in heavy medium saucepan over low heat, swirling pan occasionally, until sugar dissolves. Increase heat and boil until mixture turns rich caramel color, about 12 minutes. Let cool until slightly thickened, about 3 minutes.

Arrange some of raspberries and peaches atop cream in flower pattern. Dip fork into caramel and slowly drizzle thin threads over dessert. (*Can be prepared 20 minutes ahead and refrigerated.*) Surround meringue with remaining raspberries and peaches. Serve with raspberry sauce.

*Raspberry Sauce

Makes about 2 cups

2 10-ounce packages frozen unsweetened raspberries, thawed and drained	**¼ cup sugar** **1 tablespoon kirsch**

Push berries through fine sieve. Heat with sugar and kirsch in heavy small saucepan over low heat, swirling occasionally, until sugar dissolves. Increase heat and simmer 5 minutes. Cool, then refrigerate. (*Can be prepared 2 days ahead.*)

Broyage Torte with Strawberries

8 servings

Broyage
- **4 ounces shelled pistachios, skinned (1 cup)**
- **4 ounces hazelnuts (1 cup)**
- **1 cup (scant) sugar**
- **2½ tablespoons all purpose flour**

- **6 egg whites, room temperature**
- **¼ teaspoon cream of tartar**
  Pinch of salt

Strawberry Buttercream
- **¾ cup sugar**
- **½ cup framboise (raspberry eau-de-vie)**
- **⅓ cup water**
  Pinch of cream of tartar

- **8 egg yolks**
- **1¼ cups (2½ sticks) unsalted butter, room temperature, cut into about 20 pieces**
- **1 teaspoon vanilla**

- **8 large fresh strawberries, crushed in fine sieve (*not* pressed through), drained***
- **6 cups fresh strawberries, thinly sliced vertically**

For broyage: Preheat oven to 350°F. Line 10 × 15 × 1-inch jelly roll pan with foil; generously butter foil. Toast nuts in separate baking pans, about 5 minutes for pistachios and 8 to 10 minutes for hazelnuts, stirring occasionally. Reserve ¼ cup pistachios for garnish. Transfer remaining pistachios to processor. Rub hazelnuts in terrycloth towel 3 to 4 minutes to remove skins. Add hazelnuts, sugar and flour to pistachios and mix just until powdered, about 30 to 45 seconds.

Reduce oven temperature to 325°F. Beat egg whites in large bowl with cream of tartar and salt until stiff but not dry. Gently fold in ground nut mixture until just blended. Spread meringue evenly to edges in prepared pan; smooth top very lightly. Bake 35 minutes. Turn off oven and let broyage dry 20 minutes; do not open oven door. Remove pan from oven and cool broyage 3 minutes.

Remove entire broyage from pan with foil intact. Immediately cut broyage into three 5 × 10-inch rectangles using long sharp knife; do not use serrated knife and do not use sawing motion or layers will crumble. Carefully peel off foil. Brush away any crumbs using pastry brush. Cut off any uneven bumps and edges to level each piece. (*Broyage can be prepared 1 day ahead and stored airtight in cool dry area. Wrap each layer separately in foil.*)

For buttercream: Combine sugar, framboise, water and cream of tartar in heavy small saucepan over low heat and simmer until clear, swirling pan gently; dip pastry brush in cold water and wash down sides of pan. Increase heat to medium-high and boil syrup until thermometer registers 245°F (firm-ball stage).

Meanwhile, beat egg yolks in large bowl of electric mixer until pale and slowly dissolving ribbon forms when beaters are lifted, about 7 minutes. With mixer set at medium-low speed, very slowly pour hot syrup into yolks, being careful not to allow mixture to spatter onto sides of bowl. Increase mixer speed to medium-high and continue beating until mixture is completely cool, about 5 minutes. Add butter 1 piece at a time, beating well after each addition. Add vanilla and beat 5 more minutes; buttercream should be stiff enough to hold peaks when beaters are lifted. If too soft, refrigerate until stiffened, about 20 minutes. (*Buttercream can be prepared 1 day ahead and refrigerated.*)

Reserve about ⅓ of buttercream for top of torte. Stir crushed berries into remaining buttercream. Transfer 1 broyage layer to platter. Frost top with half of strawberry buttercream, evening edges with spatula. Arrange rows of overlapping sliced strawberries crosswise over buttercream, covering entire surface. Top with another broyage layer. Repeat frosting and berry layers. Top with remaining broyage layer. Spread reserved buttercream over top. Finely chop reserved pistachios. Sprinkle nuts in 1-inch band down center of torte. Arrange 2 rows of strawberry slices on each side of nuts. Refrigerate. Serve within 3 hours (let stand at room temperature 30 minutes before serving).

*Place sieve on paper towels after initial draining to absorb as much berry juice as possible.

Café Délice

8 to 10 servings

Meringue-Nut Layers
1⅓ cups powdered sugar, sifted
  3 ounces unblanched almonds, ground
  4 egg whites, room temperature
 ¼ teaspoon cream of tartar
 ⅛ teaspoon salt

Crème Ganache
  2 cups whipping cream

  4 ounces semisweet chocolate, broken into pieces

 ⅓ cup sugar
  2 teaspoons coffee powder (or instant coffee crystals crushed to powder)
  4 ounces sliced almonds, toasted

Position rack in lower third of oven and preheat to 225°F. Fit pastry bag with ½-inch tip. Line 12 × 18-inch baking sheet with parchment paper and trace two 8-inch circles onto paper.

For meringue layers: Mix half of powdered sugar with ground almonds in small bowl; set aside. Using electric mixer at medium speed, beat whites in large bowl until foamy. Add cream of tartar and salt, increase mixer speed and continue beating until soft peaks form. Gradually add remaining powdered sugar 1 tablespoon at a time, beating constantly until stiff peaks form. Gently fold in nut mixture. Immediately fill pastry bag with meringue.

Pipe onto parchment circles in tight spiral pattern, beginning at outer edge and working into center so no parchment shows through. Bake until firm, about 1¼ hours. Turn off oven, leave door slightly ajar and let stand until meringues are completely dry. Carefully peel off parchment paper.

For crème ganache: Combine ½ cup cream with chocolate in heavy small saucepan. Place over very low heat until chocolate is melted, stirring to blend. Remove from heat and let cool.

To assemble: Spread tops of meringue layers evenly with ganache. Whip remaining cream with sugar and coffee powder until stiff. Place 1 meringue layer on sturdy piece of cardboard and spread some of cream over ganache. Place second meringue layer on top, pressing gently so layers adhere. Spread remaining cream over top and sides. Cover cake completely with sliced almonds. Freeze. Let stand in refrigerator 1 to 2 hours before serving.

Meringues can be made 3 to 4 days ahead. To retain crispness, wrap each loosely in paper towels or waxed paper and store in cool dry place.

Mincemeat Torte with Bourbon Sauce

This recipe can be doubled.

8 servings

Meringue Layers
¾ cup plus 2 tablespoons sugar
4½ ounces (14 tablespoons) almonds, toasted
2 ounces (10 tablespoons) whole pecans, toasted
4 egg whites, room temperature
Pinch of salt
Pinch of cream of tartar

Mincemeat Buttercream
8 tablespoons sugar
6 tablespoons water

3 egg yolks, room temperature
1 cup (2 sticks) unsalted butter, room temperature
1 tablespoon instant espresso powder dissolved in 1 tablespoon warm bourbon
1 28-ounce jar mincemeat

Topping
4 egg whites, room temperature
¼ teaspoon cream of tartar
½ cup powdered sugar
Bourbon Sauce*

For meringue layers: Preheat oven to 400°F. Line 12 × 16-inch jelly roll pan with parchment, extending 1 inch beyond ends. Butter and flour paper and pan edges. Finely grind ¾ cup sugar with almonds and pecans in processor. Beat whites, salt and cream of tartar in large bowl of electric mixer to soft peaks. Beat in remaining sugar 1 tablespoon at a time until whites are stiff but not dry. Gently fold in nut mixture. Spread meringue out evenly in prepared pan. Bake until crisp and golden, about 12 minutes. Cool in pan 1 minute. Turn out onto work surface and peel off paper. Cut meringue in half lengthwise, then crosswise, forming four 6 × 8-inch rectangles. Let meringue cool to room temperature.

For buttercream: Heat 6 tablespoons sugar and 2 tablespoons water in heavy small saucepan over low heat until sugar dissolves, swirling pan occasionally. Increase heat to medium and boil until syrup turns mahogany brown, swirling pan occasionally. Stand back and carefully pour in remaining ¼ cup water (mixture may bubble up); stir until caramel dissolves. Beat yolks and remaining 2 tablespoons sugar in large bowl of electric mixer until pale yellow and slowly dissolving ribbon forms when beaters are lifted, about 6 minutes. Beat in hot syrup in thin stream until mixture is cool. Beat in butter 1 tablespoon at a time. Stir dissolved espresso into mincemeat. Fold into buttercream.

Place 1 meringue layer on ovenproof platter. Cover top evenly with ⅓ of buttercream. Continue layering, ending with meringue. Even sides and edges with spatula. (*Can be prepared 1 day ahead to this point and refrigerated, or 1 week ahead and frozen.*)

For topping: Freeze torte 1 hour. Preheat oven to 400°F. Beat whites and cream of tartar in large bowl until stiff but not dry. Sift powdered sugar over whites and beat until stiff and shiny. Spoon mixture into pastry bag and pipe decoratively over torte, covering top and sides completely. Bake until meringue is golden, about 5 minutes. Refrigerate torte at least 10 minutes. Serve with bourbon sauce. (*Can be prepared 3 hours ahead. Bring almost to room temperature before serving.*)

If doubling recipe, bake in 2 jelly roll pans. Halve layers lengthwise before assembling torte, making four 8 × 12-inch rectangles.

*Bourbon Sauce

Makes about 2 cups

4 egg yolks, room temperature	¼ cup water
¼ cup sugar	½ cup whipping cream, whipped
¼ cup bourbon	to soft peaks

Combine yolks, sugar, bourbon and water in top of double boiler set over simmering water and whisk until mixture leaves path on back of spoon when finger is drawn across, about 5 minutes. Cool to room temperature, stirring frequently. Fold in whipped cream. Pour sauce into serving pitcher. (*Sauce can be prepared 1 day ahead and refrigerated.*)

Mocha Meringues with Chocolate Ruffles

8 servings

5 egg whites, room temperature	1 tablespoon instant coffee powder dissolved in 1 tablespoon warm water
½ teaspoon fresh lemon juice or distilled white vinegar	
Pinch of salt	
1 cup superfine sugar	6 ounces semisweet chocolate, coarsely chopped
1½ cups whipping cream	
3 tablespoons coffee liqueur	24 chocolate coffee bean candies

Preheat oven to 275°F. Line 2 baking sheets with parchment. Draw eight 3-inch circles on each. Beat whites with lemon juice and salt until soft peaks form. Add sugar 1 tablespoon at a time and beat until stiff and shiny. Spoon meringue into pastry bag fitted with No. 5 star tip. Pipe rosettes or stars around circles, leaving space in center. Bake until dry and slightly colored, about 45 minutes. Remove from sheet and cool completely. Remove parchment. (*Can be prepared 1 day ahead. Store in airtight container in dry place.*)

Using electric mixer, beat cream with liqueur and coffee to stiff peaks.

Melt chocolate in double boiler over gently simmering water. Using spatula, spread thin layer of chocolate on baking sheet, smoothing back and forth to even.

Refrigerate 10 minutes. Using paint scraper or putty knife held at slight angle, push chocolate away from you quickly so chocolate folds into "ruffles." Repeat for a total of 8 ruffles. Refrigerate until ready to use.

Set 1 meringue on dessert plate. Top with another meringue. Fill center with cream. Repeat with remaining meringues. Refrigerate 30 minutes. Garnish each with chocolate ruffle and 3 chocolate coffee bean candies.

Viva Cake of Joy

Layers of nut meringue, coffee buttercream and chocolate ganache make this cake a joy to eat.

12 servings

Meringue Layers
1³/₄ cups (7 ounces) finely ground hazelnuts
1¹/₄ cups (5 ounces) finely ground almonds
1 ounce almonds, ground to powder
8 egg whites, room temperature
¹/₄ teaspoon cream of tartar
1¹/₂ cups sugar

Ganache
2 cups whipping cream
8 ounces semisweet chocolate, coarsely chopped

Coffee Buttercream
2¹/₄ cups sugar

³/₄ cup water
15 egg yolks, room temperature
3 cups (6 sticks) butter, room temperature
4¹/₂ tablespoons instant espresso powder dissolved in 1¹/₂ tablespoons hot water

1 cup well-chilled whipping cream
1 tablespoon sugar
¹/₂ teaspoon vanilla

3 ounces semisweet chocolate (garnish)

For meringue: Preheat oven to 275°F. Butter and flour 3 baking sheets. Mark 9-inch circle on each sheet, using cake pan as guide. Combine hazelnuts, almonds and almond powder in small bowl. Beat whites with cream of tartar in large bowl of electric mixer until soft peaks form. Add sugar 1 tablespoon at a time, beating until whites are stiff and shiny. Gently fold in nut mixture. Spoon into pastry bag fitted with No. 6 tip. Pipe meringue onto prepared sheets, sdtarting in center of circles and spiraling outward just to edges. Bake until crisp and golden, about 1 hour. Cool on racks.

For ganache: Bring cream to boil in heavy medium saucepan. Stir in chocolate until melted. Pour into large bowl. Refrigerate mixture until cold but not hardened, about 4 hours.

Whip chilled ganache on medium-high speed just until mixture is fluffy; *do not overbeat.* Refrigerate as necessary to attain spreadable consistency.

For buttercream: Heat 2¹/₄ cups sugar and ³/₄ cup water in heavy medium saucepan over low heat until sugar dissolves, swirling pan occcasionally. Increase heat and boil until syrup registers 250°F (hard-ball stage) on candy thermometer. Meanwhile, beat yolks in large bowl of electric mixer until pale yellow and slowly dissolving ribbon forms when beaters are lifted. Add hot syrup in thin stream and beat until cool, about 5 minutes. Mix in butter 1 tablespoon at a time. Blend coffee into buttercream in thin stream.

To assemble: Beat 1 cup cream, 1 tablespoon sugar and vanilla to soft peaks. Divide buttercream into 4 equal portions. Trim meringues to even circles. Arrange 1 meringue layer on serving platter. Spread with 1 portion of buttercream and then half of ganache and half of whipped cream. Top with second meringue layer: spread with 1 portion of buttercream and remaining ganache and whipped cream. Top with third meringue layer. spread remaining buttercream over top and sides.

Using vegetable peeler, shave 3 ounces chocolate onto waxed paper. Refrigerate until chilled. Sprinkle chocolate shavings atop cake and serve. (*Can be prepared 1 day ahead and refrigerated. Bring to room temperature before serving.*)

Cafe Metro Dacquoise

8 to 10 servings

Meringues
1 cup egg whites (about 8), room temperature
¼ teaspoon cream of tartar
1 cup sugar
1 teaspoon vanilla
1 cup ground almonds

Chocolate Buttercream
1 cup semisweet chocolate chips
½ cup whipping cream

2 cups sugar
⅔ cup water
¼ teaspoon cream of tartar
10 egg yolks, room temperature
2 cups (4 sticks) unsalted butter, room temperature, cut into pieces

Powdered sugar

1½ cups whipping cream
½ cup powdered sugar
2 tablespoons dark rum

For meringues: Preheat oven to 300°F. Butter and flour 2 large baking sheets or line with parchment paper. Trace 10-inch circle on each. Beat whites with cream of tartar in large bowl until soft peaks form. Gradually add sugar, beating until stiff peaks form. Blend in vanilla. Fold in almonds. Divide mixture between prepared baking sheets, spreading gently and evenly into two 10-inch circles. Bake until firm and light golden, about 1 to 1¼ hours. Cool briefly on baking sheet, then transfer meringues to wire racks to cool completely.

For buttercream: Combine chocolate chips and cream in small heatproof bowl. Set bowl in pan of simmering water until chocolate is melted, stirring occasionally. Let mixture cool completely.

Combine sugar, water and cream of tartar in medium saucepan over low heat. Cook until sugar dissolves, swirling pan occasionally, then increase until syrup registers 250°F on candy thermometer (hard-ball stage).

Beat yolks in large bowl of electric mixer at high speed until thick and lemon colored. Reduce mixer speed to medium and pour in hot syrup in thin stream, beating constantly until mixture is completely cool. Add butter and beat until thick and smooth, about 10 minutes. Blend in cooled chocolate mixture. Refrigerate buttercream until firm enough to pipe through pastry bag.

To assemble: Spoon buttercream into pastry bag fitted with medium star tip. Pipe ring of 1-inch-high rosettes around edge of 1 meringue round. Pipe additional rosettes of buttercream in center of meringue in shape of large X. Refrigerate.

Coat second meringue round with powdered sugar, leaving ½-inch margin at edge. Pipe ring of buttercream rosettes around edge and 1 rosette in center.

Combine cream, ½ cup powdered sugar and rum in medium bowl and whip until stiff. Fill center of first meringue with cream mixture, spreading evenly to same height as buttercream rosettes. Top with second round. Refrigerate dacquoise until ready to serve.

Market Place Marjolaine

For best flavor and texture, refrigerate the marjolaine three full days before serving.

10 servings

Meringue Layers
1²/₃ cups sliced toasted almonds
½ cup plus 2 tablespoons sugar
¼ cup all purpose flour
5 egg whites, room temperature
Pinch of salt
Pinch of cream of tartar

Almond Praline
1 cup sugar
½ cup water
1 cup sliced toasted almonds

Cream Fillings
1 cup whipping cream
2 tablespoons sugar
1 teaspoon vanilla

Chocolate Frosting
9 ounces semisweet chocolate chips
1 cup sour cream

Sifted powdered sugar

For meringue: Preheat oven to 275°F. Line bottom of 10½ × 15½-inch jelly roll pan with parchment paper. Combine almonds, sugar and flour in processor or blender and process until almonds are finely ground. Beat egg whites with salt and cream of tartar in large bowl until stiff. Gently fold in almond mixture, being careful not to deflate egg whites. Spread meringue in prepared pan. Bake until just slightly pliable, about 1 to 1¼ hours. Cool in pan 5 minutes, then transfer to rack to cool completely. Discard parchment. Wrap meringue in plastic and refrigerate overnight.

For praline: Combine sugar and water in heavy medium saucepan over low heat. Cook until sugar is dissolved, shaking pan occasionally. Increase heat and cook until sugar is caramelized and turns deep mahogany. Immediately pour mixture onto ungreased baking sheet. Cool until firm. Break into pieces and place in processor or blender. Add almonds and grind to powder. Store in container with a tight-fitting lid.

For cream fillings: Combine cream, sugar and vanilla in large bowl and whip until very stiff. Pour into strainer lined with linen towel or several layers of cheesecloth. Chill cream mixture overnight to drain.

Blend half of cream with ½ cup almond praline powder (reserve remaining praline powder for another use).

For frosting: Combine chocolate and sour cream in top of double boiler set over barely simmering water. Stir with rubber spatula just until chocolate is melted and smooth; *do not overheat or mixture will curdle.* Cool slightly. (Rewarm over hot water if frosting becomes too thick to spread.)

To assemble: Cut meringue layer crosswise into 4 equal rectangles. Place 1 rectangle on platter. Spread with praline cream. Top with second meringue layer. Spread top and sides with some of chocolate frosting. Refrigerate until chocolate sets, about 20 minutes. Spread second layer of frosting on top. Add third meringue and spread top and sides with chocolate. Refrigerate until chocolate sets. Spread with remaining cream filling. Top with fourth meringue layer. Coat top and sides of marjolaine with remaining chocolate frosting. Refrigerate until chocolate sets. Cover with plastic wrap and refrigerate at least 24 hours. Just before serving, dust top of marjolaine with sifted powdered sugar.

3 ❦ Fruit Desserts, Custards and Puddings

Gâteaux, soufflés and similarly elaborate treats make wonderful special occasion finales. But a festive meal can also reach a delightful conclusion much more simply, with a colorful fruit dessert, silky custard or creamy pudding. If you think puddings and custards are too homespun for elegant entertaining, one look through this chapter is guaranteed to convince you otherwise.

Some of these recipes combine the color and zest of fruit with opulent cream and egg mixtures. Though they are luxuriously rich, a generous complement of fresh fruit makes such desserts as Ginger Custard with Poached Pears (page 44), Raspberry Syllabub (page 46), and Strawberries in Spanish Cream (page 46) taste light and refreshing. For a real show-stopper try Pears Poached in Cabernet and Coriander with Riesling Sauce and Cornets with Chestnut Mousse (page 45)—a splendid composition of fanned pear slices, wine custard sauce and mousse-filled crisp rolled wafers. Though spectacular, it poses no problems for the cook because all of the components can be prepared a day ahead.

Those renowned English classics, Plum Pudding (page 52) and Trifle (page 49), are quintessential holiday treats. Perhaps less familiar to American cooks is the trio of Italian favorites: ultra-rich Tiramisù (page 47), Gianduia with Zabaglione (page 50), and trifle's Mediterranean cousin, Zuppa Inglese (page 48). You will find them wonderful discoveries: All are easy to make but superbly elegant and satisfying.

Oranges in Tangerine Sauce

*Perfect for rounding out
an oriental menu.*

6 servings

1 cup fresh tangerine juice
3 tablespoons sugar
1 teaspoon grenadine syrup
1 3-inch piece vanilla bean, split
3 tablespoons orange liqueur

6 large seedless oranges, peel and
  white pith removed

Candied Orange Peel*

Simmer juice, sugar, syrup and vanilla bean in heavy small nonaluminum saucepan until liquid is reduced to ½ cup. Stir in liqueur. Pour over oranges. Cool completely. Cover and chill overnight. (*Can be prepared 2 days ahead.*)

To serve, arrange oranges in goblets. Spoon sauce over. Garnish with peel.

*Candied Orange Peel

Makes about ½ cup

2 large oranges
½ cup water

⅓ cup powdered sugar
2 teaspoons grenadine syrup

Remove peel from oranges. Cut peel into 1/16-inch-wide strips. Boil peel, water, sugar and syrup in heavy small saucepan until peel is tender and liquid is thick and syrupy, about 15 minutes. Let cool completely. (*Can be prepared 2 weeks ahead and refrigerated.*)

Ginger Custard with Poached Pears

12 to 14 servings

Poached Pears
  12 cups water
   3 cups sugar
   2 tablespoons fresh lemon juice
   1 teaspoon finely grated lemon peel
   2 3-inch cinnamon sticks
  10 medium pears, halved and cored

Ginger Custard
   5 cups whipping cream
   6 tablespoons sugar
  10 egg yolks, room temperature

1 tablespoon vanilla
Pinch of salt

½ cup cooked rice (without salt)
½ cup finely chopped crystallized
  ginger

1¼ cups firmly packed light brown
  sugar
½ cup whipping cream
Mint leaves or candied violets

For pears: Combine all ingredients except pears in 6-quart pot and cook over low heat until sugar dissolves, swirling pot occasionally. Add pears. Increase heat so liquid is barely shaking. Poach pears until just tender when pierced with tip of sharp knife, about 10 minutes (time will vary depending on ripeness of pears). Cool pears in poaching liquid. (*Custard can be prepared 2 days ahead, covered and refrigerated.*) Drain pears. Reserve 6 halves. Cut remaining halves into ½-inch dice. Drain in colander; pat dry.

For custard: Scald 5 cups cream in heavy large saucepan. Remove from heat. Add sugar and stir until dissolved. Whisk yolks with vanilla and salt in bowl. Gradually whisk in cream.

Preheat oven to 300°F. Sprinkle diced pears, rice and ginger in 12 × 7½ × 2-inch ovenproof glass or ceramic dish. Stir in cream mixture. Set dish in shallow pan. Pour enough simmering water into pan to come 1½ inches up sides of dish. Bake until knife inserted in center of custard comes out clean, about 50 minutes. Cool to room temperature. Cover and refrigerate 8 hours or overnight.

Preheat broiler. Press brown sugar through strainer onto top of custard. Broil 6 to 8 inches from heat until sugar melts, watching carefully, 2 to 3 minutes. Cool several minutes. Refrigerate at least 30 minutes. (*Custard can be prepared 1 day ahead.*)

Pat reserved pear halves dry. Cut each half lengthwise into thin slices. Create 6 fans at equidistant points on top of custard. (Do not decorate more than 30 minutes before serving.)

Beat ½ cup cream to stiff peaks. Spoon into pastry bag fitted with star tip. Pipe rosettes on narrow point of each fanned pear half. Place mint leaf or candied violet in center of each rosette. Serve immediately.

Pears Poached in Cabernet and Coriander with Riesling Sauce and Cornets with Chestnut Mousse

Poach the pears one day in advance to enhance the special flavor that comes from the large amount of coriander.

4 servings

Poached Pears
1 750-ml bottle Cabernet Sauvignon
1 cup sugar
14 tablespoons ground coriander
2 medium pears, peeled, halved and cored

Riesling Sauce
6 egg yolks, room temperature
½ cup sugar
1½ cups Riesling

Cornets
7 tablespoons sugar
2 egg whites, room temperature
11 tablespoons all purpose flour
2 tablespoons (¼ stick) unsalted butter, melted and cooled

Chestnut Mousse
6 tablespoons whipping cream, whipped to soft peaks
5 tablespoons (3 ounces) chestnut spread (*crème de marrons*)

For pears: Heat wine, sugar and coriander in heavy medium saucepan over low heat until sugar dissolves, swirling pan occasionally. Increase heat and bring to simmer. Add pears and poach until tender when pierced with knife, about 8 minutes. Cool. Refrigerate overnight, turning occasionally.

For sauce: Beat yolks and sugar in large bowl of electric mixer until pale yellow and slowly dissolving ribbon forms when beaters are lifted, about 6 minutes. Meanwhile, bring Riesling to boil in heavy large saucepan. Slowly beat into yolks. Return mixture to pan and stir over medium-low heat until thick enough to coat spoon; *do not boil.* Pour into bowl. Cool, then cover and refrigerate. (*Can be prepared 1 day ahead.*)

For cornets: Preheat oven to 325°F. Butter 2 baking sheets and dust with flour. Mark 5-inch circles in flour, spacing ½ inch apart. Whisk sugar and whites to blend. Mix in flour and butter. Place 1 tablespoon batter in center of each circle. Spread out to edges of circles, using metal spatula. Bake 1 sheet at a time until cookies are just beginning to color, about 7 minutes. Quickly remove cookies with large spatula and curl into cornet shapes. (If cookies become too stiff to shape, return to oven briefly to soften.) Cool on racks. (*Can be prepared 1 day ahead and stored in airtight container.*)

For mousse: Gently fold whipped cream into chestnut spread. Cover and refrigerate. (*Can be prepared 1 day ahead.*)

To assemble: Drain pears and pat dry with paper towels. Cut crosswise into ⅛-inch slices. Fan out each pear half on individual plates. Pour Riesling sauce at base of each pear fan. Spoon chestnut mousse into pastry bag fitted with star tip and pipe into 4 cornets. Place 1 cornet on each plate with point at base of fan. Serve immediately.

Raspberry Syllabub

6 to 8 servings

1 to 1½ pounds fresh raspberries
½ cup superfine sugar
¼ cup brandy

1½ cups well-chilled whipping cream
Rolled wafer cookies

Set aside 12 to 16 raspberries. Combine remaining raspberries, sugar and brandy in bowl. Cover and refrigerate 2 to 3 hours.

Drain raspberries, reserving liquid. Mash raspberries gently. Drain berries again, reserving liquid. Beat cream to stiff peaks. Fold in mashed raspberries. Divide reserved liquids among goblets. Spoon or pipe raspberry cream over top. Decorate with reserved berries. Refrigerate until firm. Serve with wafers.

Molded Raspberry Cake

A creamy, colorful finale.

8 to 10 servings

8 10-ounce packages frozen raspberries in syrup, defrosted

3 3-ounce packages ladyfingers, split in half (36 whole ladyfingers)

Orange liqueur

1 pint (2 cups) whipping cream
¼ cup orange liqueur
1 ounce candied violets

Drain raspberries in strainer 1 hour, shaking strainer occasionally.

Lightly brush ladyfingers with liqueur. Line bottom and sides of 9 × 5-inch glass loaf pan or 12 × 4 × 2½-inch bread pan with some of ladyfingers, sugared side out. Spoon ⅓ of raspberries over bottom layer. Top with another layer of ladyfingers. Repeat twice to fill pan. Fold tips of ladyfingers lining sides over top and press gently but firmly to make cake compact. Cover tightly with foil so pan can be turned over and cake will remain intact. Refrigerate 6 to 8 hours, turning pan over 2 or 3 times.

When ready to serve, remove foil and turn cake out onto serving platter. Whip cream with ¼ cup liqueur until quite stiff and spread heavily over top and sides. Decorate with candied violets.

Strawberries in Spanish Cream

6 servings

3 eggs
½ cup sugar
⅓ cup cream Sherry
3 tablespoons fresh lemon juice, strained
¼ teaspoon vanilla
½ cup (1 stick) unsalted butter, cut into 8 pieces

1 10-ounce package unsweetened frozen strawberries, thawed
1 quart fresh strawberries with stems

Beat eggs and sugar in heavy large saucepan until pale and thick. Stir in Sherry, lemon juice and vanilla. Place over medium-low heat. Whisk in butter 1 piece at a time and cook until Spanish cream thickens, stirring constantly, 5 to 8 minutes; do not boil. Cool completely; do not refrigerate.

Puree thawed strawberries in blender. Strain to remove seeds. Spoon thin pool of Spanish cream onto dessert plate. Spoon strawberry puree into pastry bag fitted with smallest plain tip. Pipe 2 fine concentric circles of puree onto cream. Using small knife and starting at center, cut 8 equidistant lines through puree and cream to form spiderweb design. Arrange fresh strawberries in center and serve immediately.

Coconut Flan

8 servings

1½ cups sugar
3 tablespoons water

4 cups milk
¾ cup shredded coconut
1 vanilla bean, split lengthwise
Peel of 1 lemon, cut into strips

5 egg yolks
4 eggs
2 tablespoons brandy

¼ cup toasted shredded coconut

Combine ¾ cup sugar with 3 tablespoons water in medium saucepan over medium-low heat and cook until sugar is melted and syrup is medium brown. Immediately pour syrup into 9 × 2-inch heavy round cake pan or 1½- to 2-quart fluted mold. With mitts on both hands, rotate pan gently, swirling syrup to form even layer on bottom and sides; rotate pan until syrup is almost set. Invert over rack until set.

Preheat oven to 350°F. Combine milk, coconut, vanilla bean and lemon peel in medium saucepan and bring to boil over medium heat. Remove from heat, cover and let steep 10 to 15 minutes.

Remove vanilla bean and lemon peel. Combine egg yolks and whole eggs in large bowl of electric mixer. Gradually add remaining ¾ cup sugar to egg mixture, beating until light and foamy. Whisk hot milk mixture into eggs in slow steady stream, whisking constantly to prevent curdling (mixture will be foamy). Strain into large bowl through sieve lined with 2 layers of moistened cheesecloth. Stir in brandy.

Pour into prepared mold. Set mold in large shallow pan. Add enough boiling water to pan to come halfway up sides of mold. Transfer to oven and immediately reduce temperature to 325°F.

Bake until tester inserted in center comes out clean, about 40 minutes. Cool to room temperature. Refrigerate several hours or overnight.

To serve, rewarm flan quickly over low heat to loosen from pan if necessary. Invert onto rimmed shallow platter. Sprinkle toasted coconut over top.

Tiramisù

A traditional Italian dessert from Los Angeles's Rex–Il Ristorante.

8 servings

1 cup sugar
4 egg yolks, room temperature
1½ teaspoons vanilla
8 to 9 ounces mascarpone cheese,*
   room temperature

2 cups whipping cream

½ cup strong espresso
2 to 3 teaspoons grappa brandy
40 ladyfingers

1 cup whipping cream, whipped to
   stiff peaks
4 ounces semisweet chocolate

Mix sugar and egg yolks in large bowl of electric mixer at low speed 2 minutes. Add vanilla, increase speed to high and beat until mixture is pale yellow and forms slowly dissolving ribbon when beaters are lifted, about 5 minutes. Reduce speed to low and blend in cheese 1 tablespoon at a time, mixing well after each addition. Increase speed to medium and beat until slightly thickened and smooth, 1 to 2 minutes. Cover and refrigerate until thickened, about 45 minutes.

Whip 2 cups cream in large bowl to soft peaks. Gently fold cream into chilled cheese mixture. Return filling to refrigerator and chill well.

To assemble: Cut piece of cardboard into 4 × 11-inch rectangle. Position long edge of cardboard parallel to work surface in front of you. Blend espresso with grappa in small bowl. Dip rounded side of ladyfingers into espresso mixture one at a time, arranging ladyfingers side by side across length of cardboard. Spread ¼-inch-thick layer of filling over ladyfingers. Arrange 3 rows of dipped ladyfingers, alternating direction of ladyfingers. Smooth sides with spatula.

To decorate: Spoon whipped cream into pastry bag fitted with star tip. Pipe cream in perpendicular bands around entire cake, then pipe rippled border around top edge. Shave chocolate over piece of waxed paper. Lift sides to form pouring spout at one end. Sprinkle chocolate decoratively on top of cake. Refrigerate. Let cake stand at room temperature 30 minutes before serving.

*An Italian double cream cheese, available at cheese shops.

Luciano's Zuppa Inglese

From San Francisco's Ristorante da Luciano.

8 servings

7 eggs, separated, room temperature
¾ cup superfine sugar
⅓ cup sifted all purpose flour
2 cups milk
2 1-inch pieces vanilla bean, split and scraped

1 10-inch round sponge cake
Rosolio or Cherry Heering liqueur

12 almond macaroons
Amaretto liqueur
2 tablespoons sweetened cocoa powder
8 ladyfingers, halved lengthwise

3 tablespoons sugar

Whisk yolks and ¾ cup superfine sugar in large bowl until light and lemon colored. Blend in flour. Combine milk and vanilla bean in heavy medium saucepan. Bring just to boil over medium heat. Add yolk mixture and whisk vigorously 30 seconds. Remove from heat. Remove vanilla bean. Cool pastry cream completely.

Cut about ¼-inch-thick layer of sponge cake using long serrated knife. Set in bottom of 10-inch round ovenproof glass dish with 2-inch rim. Brush generously with cherry liqueur. Spread with 1 cup pastry cream. Dip macaroons in amaretto and arrange over pastry cream. Mix 1 cup of remaining pastry cream and cocoa powder in small bowl. Spread over macaroons. Top with ladyfinger halves. Brush generously with cherry liqueur. Spread with remaining 1 cup pastry cream. Cover with another ¼-inch-thick layer of sponge cake, making sure all pastry cream is covered. Brush cake generously with amaretto.

Preheat oven to 450°F. Beat whites with 3 tablespoons sugar until stiff peaks form. Spread most of meringue onto sides and top of cake, sealing completely. Spoon remainder into pastry bag fitted with medium tip and pipe decoratively over top. Bake until light brown, 40 to 50 *seconds*. Serve immediately.

English Trifle

The ideal do-ahead dessert for Christmas dinner. The recipe requires three batches of custard; for best results, prepare each batch separately to avoid burning or lumping.

10 servings

36 1½-inch almond macaroons
⅓ to ½ cup amaretto
1 12-ounce jar seedless red raspberry jam

Custard (makes 1¼ cups)
4 egg yolks
3 tablespoons sugar
½ cup plus 2 tablespoons milk
¼ cup whipping cream
2½ teaspoons cornstarch dissolved in 2 tablespoons milk
½ teaspoon vanilla
⅛ teaspoon freshly grated nutmeg

1 12-ounce pound cake, cut into ¼-inch slices (about 16 to 17)
½ to ⅔ cup cream Sherry
4 10-ounce packages frozen raspberries, thawed and thoroughly drained

2 cups (1 pint) whipping cream
2 tablespoons sugar
½ teaspoon vanilla or to taste

Brush flat side of 12 to 15 macaroons with liqueur. Arrange flat sides around sides of 12-cup glass bowl, then line bottom flat side up. Spread generously with red raspberry jam, being careful not to crush macaroons.

For custard: Whisk yolks in medium saucepan. Gradually add sugar, whisking until mixture is thick and lemon colored, about 1 to 2 minutes. Blend in milk, whipping cream and cornstarch mixture. Place over medium-low heat and cook, stirring constantly, until mixture thickens, about 3 to 5 minutes (*do not boil or mixture will separate*). Remove from heat and stir until slightly cooled. Blend in vanilla and nutmeg. Transfer to bowl. Repeat twice to make 3¾ cups custard.

Spoon 1¼ cups custard over raspberry jam layer. Cover with single layer of pound cake slices. Using pastry brush, soak cake generously with ¼ to ⅓ cup Sherry. Spread thin layer of raspberry jam over cake. Top with half of drained raspberries. Carefully spoon another 1¼ cups custard over berries. Repeat layering with remaining pound cake slices, Sherry and jam. Cover with remaining berries. Carefully spread remaining custard over top.

Brush 8 or 9 macaroons with liqueur and arrange over custard flat side down. Place plastic wrap directly on surface of trifle. Refrigerate overnight. (*Can be prepared up to 2 days ahead.*)

About 3 to 4 hours before serving, whip cream in medium bowl until foamy. Add sugar and vanilla and continue beating until stiff but not dry. Spoon over macaroons, swirling top. Crush 10 to 12 macaroons. Sprinkle 1-inch border around outer edge of cream. Refrigerate until serving time.

Crème Edinburgh

8 servings

¾ cup firmly packed dark brown sugar
2½ tablespoons unsalted butter
2½ cups whipping cream, scalded

10 egg yolks, room temperature
½ teaspoon vanilla
Pinch of salt
Unsweetened whipped cream

Preheat oven to 300°F. Combine brown sugar and butter in heavy medium saucepan and stir to blend. Place over medium heat until melted. Remove from heat; gradually mix in hot cream.

Combine yolks, vanilla and salt in large bowl of electric mixer and beat at high speed until mixture forms slowly dissolving ribbon when beaters are lifted, about 5 minutes. Gradually beat in cream mixture. Strain into eight 4-ounce ramekins. Set in roasting pan. Add enough hot water to pan to come halfway up sides of ramekins. Bake until tops of custards are puffed and light golden, 20 to 25 minutes. Cool, then chill. Pipe rosette of whipped cream onto each custard just before serving.

Gianduia with Zabaglione

This chocolate amaretti pudding is a Piedmontese specialty. Prepare the rich zabaglione just before serving.

12 servings

Gianduia
- 1/2 cup (1 stick) butter
- 2 cups finely crushed amaretti (8 ounces)
- 2/3 cup all purpose flour
- 2/3 cup unsweetened cocoa powder (preferably Dutch process)
- 1/2 cup sugar
- 4 cups (1 quart) milk

Zabaglione
- 1/4 cup sugar
- 4 egg yolks, room temperature
- 1/2 cup dry Marsala

Toasted slivered almonds

For gianduia: Melt butter in heavy large saucepan over low heat. Add cookie crumbs and mix well. Blend in flour, cocoa and sugar. Gradually stir in milk. Cook to very thick pudding consistency, about 30 minutes, stirring almost constantly. Pour into bowl; cool. Refrigerate several hours.

For zabaglione: Combine sugar and yolks in top of double boiler (off heat) and whisk until pale yellow and slowly dissolving ribbon forms when whisk is lifted, about 7 minutes. Bring water in bottom of double boiler to simmer. Set yolk mixture over (but not touching) simmering water. Add Marsala to yolks and beat until mixture thickens and forms soft mounds.

To serve, spoon gianduia into individual bowls. Top with zabaglione. Sprinkle with almonds and serve.

Gingerbread Crème Brûlée

12 servings

Gingerbread
- 2/3 cup firmly packed brown sugar
- 10 tablespoons (1 1/4 sticks) unsalted butter, room temperature
- 4 egg yolks, room temperature
- 2/3 cup dark molasses
- 1/3 cup warm water
- 1 1/2 teaspoons baking soda
- 2 1/3 cups cake flour
- 5 teaspoons ground ginger
- 1/2 teaspoon freshly grated nutmeg
- 1/2 teaspoon cinnamon
- 1/2 teaspoon ground allspice
- 1/2 teaspoon salt
- 6 egg whites, room temperature
- 1/4 teaspoon cream of tartar
- 3 tablespoons plus 2 teaspoons sugar

Custard
- 1 ounce fresh ginger, peeled and cut into 1/2-inch slices
- 3 cups whipping cream
- 1 vanilla bean, halved lengthwise
- 2 tablespoons sour cream
- 7 egg yolks, room temperature
- 15 tablespoons sugar

For gingerbread: Preheat oven to 350°F. Butter and flour 10 1/2 × 15 1/2-inch jelly roll pan. Cream brown sugar with butter in electric mixer bowl until light. Beat in yolks one at a time. Combine molasses, 1/3 cup warm water and baking soda and blend into butter mixture. Sift flour, spices and salt together twice. Fold into batter. Beat whites and cream of tartar in another large bowl to soft peaks. Add 3 tablespoons sugar 1 tablespoon at a time and beat until whites are stiff but not dry. Gently fold 1/3 of whites into batter, then fold in remaining whites. Spread batter evenly in prepared pan. Bake until springy to touch, 15 to 20 minutes. Cool completely in pan.

Sprinkle cake with remaining 2 teaspoons sugar. Invert onto work surface. Cut cake rounds to fit bottoms of twelve 6-ounce broilerproof straight-sided dishes, using dishes as guide. Trim cake rounds to ½-inch thickness. Place cake rounds in dishes.

For custard: Blanch ginger in saucepan of boiling water 1 minute; drain. Pour cream into heavy medium saucepan. Scrape vanilla seeds into cream; add pod, blanched ginger and sour cream. Bring to boil over medium heat, stirring occasionally. Meanwhile, combine yolks and 7 tablespoons sugar in top of double boiler set over almost simmering water. Whisk until warm and consistency of mayonnaise, about 6 minutes, scraping down sides of bowl occasionally. Slowly pour hot cream mixture into yolks, whisking constantly. Cook over simmering water until mixture coats back of spoon without dripping off, about 35 minutes, whisking occasionally. (Do not let water get too hot or custard will curdle.) Strain custard through fine sieve into large bowl. Immediately divide custard among cake-lined dishes. Cool at least 15 minutes.

Preheat broiler. Sprinkle 2 teaspoons sugar atop each custard. Broil desserts 2 inches from heat (in batches if necessary) until sugar turns light brown, watching carefully, about 2 minutes. Cool, then refrigerate at least 1 hour. Let stand at room temperature 15 minutes before serving. (*Can be prepared 1 day ahead. Wrap tightly before refrigerating.*)

Gâteau de Riz

16 servings

2 cups milk
3½ tablespoons long-grain rice (2 ounces)
2 tablespoons sugar

Bavarian Cream
1 cup milk
4 egg yolks
¼ cup sugar
1 teaspoon unflavored gelatin

½ teaspoon vanilla
4 cups (1 quart) whipping cream

3 cups candied fruit, coarsely chopped

3 medium-size fresh peaches or other seasonal fruit, peeled, halved and pitted
1 cup (about) apricot jam, melted and cooled

Combine 2 cups milk, rice and 2 tablespoons sugar in medium saucepan and bring just to simmer over medium-high heat. Reduce heat and simmer gently until liquid is absorbed and rice is tender, 1 hour, stirring occasionally.

Meanwhile, prepare cream: Bring 1 cup milk to boil in medium saucepan. Place yolks in large bowl of electric mixer. Gradually beat in ¼ cup sugar and continue beating until mixture is pale yellow and forms slowly dissolving ribbon when beaters are lifted, about 5 to 6 minutes. Gradually add half of hot milk, beating constantly. Pour mixture back into saucepan. Stir over low heat 1 minute to rewarm. Whisk in gelatin, stirring until completely dissolved. Transfer to large bowl. Set custard aside to cool.

Lightly butter 9-inch springform pan. Set medium bowl in large bowl of ice to chill. Stir vanilla into rice mixture. Gently fold cream mixture into cooled custard. Pour into prepared springform. Refrigerate for 6 hours.

Remove springform. Transfer dessert to platter. Set 1 peach half in center. Thinly slice remaining peaches and arrange around peach half in center, overlapping slightly. Brush entire surface of dessert with jam and serve.

English Plum Pudding

10 to 12 servings

3/4 cup brandy (or more)
4 ounces beef suet, ground
2 1/2 cups fresh fine breadcrumbs
1 1/4 cups firmly packed light
    brown sugar
1 1/4 cups golden raisins
1 1/4 cups dark raisins
1 1/4 cups dried currants
3/4 cup glacéed cherries
3/4 cup slivered almonds
1/2 cup glacéed lemon peel
1/2 cup glacéed orange peel
1/2 cup all purpose flour
2 eggs, beaten to blend

1 small tart green apple, peeled,
    cored and grated
Grated peel of 1 orange
3 tablespoons molasses
1 teaspoon ground allspice
1 teaspoon cinnamon
1 teaspoon baking soda
1/2 teaspoon ground cloves
1/2 teaspoon salt
1/4 teaspoon freshly grated nutmeg

Holly sprig (garnish)
Hard Sauce*

Butter 2-quart pudding mold. Add water to large steamer to within 1 inch of rack. Cover and bring to boil over medium-high heat (do not let boiling water touch rack). Meanwhile, combine 1/2 cup brandy with all remaining ingredients (except garnish and sauce) in large bowl and mix thoroughly. Turn mixture into prepared mold. Cover with foil and tie tightly with string. Reduce heat to medium-low, carefully remove steamer cover and set mold on rack. Cover and steam 4 hours, adding water occasionally to steamer as necessary. Store at room temperature at least 3 months, adding drops of brandy or rum to pudding about once a week to moisten.

To serve, resteam pudding in same manner 1 hour. Invert pudding onto rimmed serving dish. Heat remaining 1/4 cup brandy in small saucepan. Pour over pudding and ignite. Garnish with holly sprig. Pass sauce separately.

*Hard Sauce

Makes about 1 cup

1/2 cup (1 stick) unsalted butter,
    room temperature
1/2 cup powdered sugar

1/8 teaspoon freshly grated nutmeg
2 tablespoons dark rum or brandy
1 teaspoon vanilla

Cream butter in medium bowl. Beat in powdered sugar and nutmeg. Blend in rum and vanilla. Chill until firm.

4 ❦ Frozen Desserts

If you scream for ice cream you will cheer for the recipes in this chapter. Here, ice cream is just the beginning—most of these desserts are dressed up with plenty of added attractions.

Consider, for example, Almond Amaretto Alaska (page 54): a layer of light almond- and lemon-scented cake is spread with cherry-amaretto glaze, topped with homemade almond ice cream and swirled with meringue. Even more spectacular, Poached Apples with Cider Sorbet and Caramel Dome (page 55) are composed of sorbet-filled poached apple halves surrounded with a pool of creamy sauce and enclosed in a golden cage of caramel. Black Orchid Puffs Flambé (page 56) make a dramatic impression that belies their ease of preparation. And if chocolate is your weakness, you might choose Frozen Fudge Supreme (page 59), Frozen Chocolate Rum Sponge Roll with Hot Fudge Sauce (page 61), or—for the truly incorrigible—Quadruple Chocolate Suicide (page 59).

Winter or summer, a frozen dessert is always a refreshing conclusion to a rich meal. And the best part is that it is do-ahead; last-minute preparation rarely involves anything more complicated than drizzling on a sauce or shaving a few decorative chocolate curls.

Almond Amaretto Alaska

8 to 10 servings

Ice Cream
 5 cups whipping cream
 7½ ounces (1⅓ cups) blanched almonds, toasted and coarsely chopped
 1 vanilla bean, split
 8 egg yolks
 1 cup sugar
 ½ teaspoon almond extract

 1 tablespoon amaretto

Cake
 ½ medium lemon
 2 ounces (⅓ cup) blanched almonds, toasted
 ¼ cup plus 2 tablespoons sugar
 2 eggs

 1 teaspoon vanilla
 ½ cup cake flour
 ½ teaspoon baking powder
 3 tablespoons butter, melted and cooled

Glaze
 ½ cup cherry preserves
 1 tablespoon amaretto

Meringue
 6 egg whites, room temperature
 ½ teaspoon cream of tartar
 1 cup sugar
 1 teaspoon vanilla

 2 tablespoons amaretto
 Sliced almonds

For ice cream: Combine cream, almonds and vanilla bean in heavy large saucepan and bring to boil. Reduce heat and simmer 25 minutes. Remove from heat and let stand 15 minutes. Strain cream into bowl, pressing on almonds with back of spoon to extract as much liquid as possible. Discard almonds and vanilla bean. Whisk yolks with sugar in heavy large saucepan until thick and pale. Whisk in cream. Using wooden spoon, stir mixture over medium-low heat until thickened and candy thermometer registers 175°F. Let cool to room temperature. Blend in almond extract. Cover and refrigerate until very cold. Turn custard into ice cream maker and freeze according to manufacturer's instructions.

Line 8-inch springform pan with plastic wrap. Stir amaretto into ice cream. Spoon into pan, spreading evenly. Press piece of plastic wrap onto surface of ice cream. Cover tightly with foil. Freeze until hard, about 24 hours.

For cake: Position rack in center of oven and preheat to 350°F. Butter and flour 8-inch cake pan. Remove lemon peel (yellow part only) using vegetable peeler. Finely grind peel and almonds with ¼ cup sugar in processor. Beat eggs and remaining sugar in large bowl of electric mixer until light and fluffy. Blend in vanilla. Sift together flour and baking powder. Fold almond mixture, flour mixture and melted butter alternately into egg mixture; do not overfold. Pour batter into prepared pan. Bake until tester inserted in center comes out clean, about 20 minutes. Invert onto rack and cool completely.

For glaze: Heat preserves and amaretto in heavy saucepan over low heat until preserves melt, stirring occasionally.

For meringue: Beat whites in large bowl of electric mixer until frothy. Add cream of tartar and beat until soft peaks form. Add sugar 1 tablespoon at a time and beat until whites are stiff but not dry. Blend in vanilla.

To assemble: Preheat oven to 425°F. Using toothpick, pierce top of cake. Sprinkle with 2 tablespoons amaretto. Set cake on large ovenproof platter. Spread with glaze. Carefully remove springform from ice cream. Peel off plastic wrap. Set ice cream atop cake. Immediately frost with all but 1 cup meringue, covering ice cream completely. Spoon 1 cup meringue into pastry bag fitted with small star tip. Pipe rosettes decoratively over Alaska. Sprinkle with sliced almonds. Bake until top begins to brown, about 3 minutes. Serve immediately.

Poached Apples with Cider Sorbet and Caramel Dome

Exciting flavors and textures—complemented by a luscious sauce.

8 servings

Poached Apples
4¹/₂ cups sugar
  2 cups water
  ¹/₄ cup fresh lemon juice
  4 extra-large Rhode Island Greening, Granny Smith or Golden Delicious apples, peeled, halved and cored

Caramel Sauce
  ³/₄ cup whipping cream

  ¹/₄ cup sour cream
  ¹/₄ cup half and half

Caramel Domes
  1 cup sugar
  ¹/₃ cup water
  2 tablespoons light corn syrup
    Pinch of cream of tartar

    Hazelnut oil, almond oil or nonstick vegetable oil spray

    Cider Sorbet*
    Mint sprigs (optional garnish)

For apples: Heat sugar, water and lemon juice in heavy large skillet over low heat, swirling pan occasionally, until sugar dissolves. Increase heat and boil until candy thermometer registers 310°F (hard-crack stage), about 25 minutes. Add apples, reduce heat and simmer until apples are crisp-tender, basting constantly, about 7 minutes. Transfer apples to rack, using slotted spoon. Reserve ¹/₂ cup cooking syrup for sauce. Wrap apples and refrigerate 2 hours. (*Can be prepared 1 day ahead.*)

For sauce: Heat ¹/₂ cup reserved apple cooking syrup and cream in heavy small saucepan over low heat, whisking until syrup dissolves. Cool.

Whisk sour cream into sauce, then half and half. Refrigerate at least 1 hour. (*Can be prepared 1 day ahead.*)

For domes: Heat sugar, water, corn syrup and cream of tartar in heavy medium saucepan over low heat, swirling pan occasionally, until sugar dissolves. Increase heat and boil until candy thermometer registers 310°F (hard-crack stage), about 20 minutes. Set pan in larger pan filled with ice cubes.

Grease exterior of 4-inch-diameter round-bottomed bowl with nut oil or vegetable spray. Reheat syrup until it falls from spoon in very heavy thread (about 230°F). Remove from heat. Dip fork into syrup and draw threads of syrup back and forth across prepared bowl, forming lattice dome. Cool until caramel starts to harden and is just warm to touch. Gently push on bottom edge of dome until it loosens from bowl. Turn bowl over and carefully push off dome. Repeat to form 8 domes, warming syrup to soften as necessary. (*Can be prepared 1 day ahead to this point. Store domes in airtight container.*)

To assemble: Let apples and sauce stand at room temperature 10 minutes. Place scoop of sorbet in center of each apple half; invert onto plates. Spoon sauce around apples. Cover each apple with dome. Garnish with mint and serve.

*Cider Sorbet

Makes about 2 cups

13 ounces Rhode Island Greening apples, peeled, quartered and cored
³/₄ cup plus 2 tablespoons sparkling apple cider

¹/₂ cup sugar
2¹/₂ tablespoons (about) fresh lemon juice

Combine apples, cider and sugar in blender and puree until smooth. Strain through fine sieve. Add lemon juice to taste. Process apple mixture in ice cream maker according to manufacturer's instructions. Transfer to covered container and freeze until firm, at least 2 hours.

Black Orchid Puffs Flambé

Makes 12

1½ quarts vanilla ice cream, softened
5 tablespoons blackberry brandy
3 tablespoons white crème de cacao
12 unfilled baked cream puffs

Black Raspberry Sauce
2 cups fresh or unsweetened frozen raspberries, thawed and drained

1 cup seedless black raspberry preserves

Powdered sugar
¼ cup blackberry brandy, warmed

Combine ice cream, brandy and crème de cacao in large bowl. Cover and freeze until firm, several hours or overnight. Slice ⅔ across top of each cream puff. Lift tops and fill puffs with ice cream mixture, packing tightly. Close tops, wrap each puff in foil and freeze until ready to serve.

For sauce: Combine raspberries and preserves in blender or processor and mix until smooth. Press through strainer to remove seeds. Warm strained sauce in small saucepan over medium-low heat.

To serve, arrange filled puffs on dessert plates. Sprinkle with powdered sugar. Add ¼ cup blackberry brandy to sauce and ignite. Spoon flaming sauce over puffs and serve immediately.

Caramel Mousse with Butterscotch Sauce

6 servings

Mousse
¾ cup sugar
½ cup boiling water

4 egg yolks, room temperature

1½ cups whipping cream
½ teaspoon vanilla

Sauce
¼ cup firmly packed brown sugar
¼ cup sugar

¼ cup dark corn syrup
¼ cup whipping cream
2 tablespoons (¼ stick) butter
Pinch of salt
½ teaspoon vanilla

For mousse: Cook sugar in heavy 2-quart saucepan over low heat, without stirring, until rich mahogany color, swirling pan occasionally and watching carefully, about 20 minutes. Using long-handled spoon, gradually stir in boiling water (be careful; mixture may spatter). Cook until caramel dissolves, about 4 minutes.

Meanwhile, using electric mixer, beat yolks until thick and light. Gradually beat in caramel and continue beating until mixture begins to cool. Let cool to room temperature.

Beat cream with vanilla to soft peaks. Fold cream into caramel mixture. Divide among six 1-cup molds, filling about ¾ full. Cover mousse and freeze until firm.

For sauce: Combine all ingredients except vanilla in heavy small saucepan and simmer 5 minutes. Let cool 3 minutes. Blend in vanilla. Spoon sauce over caramel mousse in molds and serve immediately.

Raspberry Cheesecake Japonaise

Le Chantilly

Irwin Horowitz

English Trifle

Irwin Horowitz

*Clockwise from top:
Derby Dacquoise Cake;
Chunky Chocolate Loaf;
Frozen Honey Orange
Cream; Chestnut Choco-
late Cake*

Left: Café Délice
Right: Coffee Cream Cake

Irwin Horowitz

Pear Charlotte with Raspberry Sauce

Cranberry-Cassis Mousse

Makes 2½ quarts

8 egg yolks
1 cup cranberry juice cocktail

4 cups freshly cooked sweetened cranberries, cooled and well drained
⅓ cup crème de cassis

1 cup whipping cream
4 egg whites
½ cup sugar

Cassis Sauce
1 cup cranberry juice cocktail
¼ cup water
1 tablespoon arrowroot
1 cup freshly cooked sweetened cranberries, cooled and well drained
¼ cup crème de cassis

Beat egg yolks in large mixing bowl until thick and lemon colored. Add cranberry juice and continue beating until well blended. Transfer to large saucepan and cook over medium heat, stirring constantly, until mixture thickens and coats spoon heavily (do not boil or yolks will curdle). Remove from heat and let custard cool completely.

Add 4 cups cranberries to cooled custard and blend well. Transfer to large bowl. Chill until mixture begins to thicken, about 30 minutes. Add ⅓ cup crème de cassis and mix thoroughly.

Whip cream in medium bowl until stiff. Beat egg whites in another bowl until foamy. Gradually add sugar to whites, beating until soft peaks form. Gently fold cream into cranberry mixture with spatula; then gently fold in egg whites until completely blended. Pour mixture into decorative 2½-quart mold or soufflé dish. Cover with foil and freeze until firm.

For sauce: Bring cranberry juice to simmer in medium saucepan over low heat. Combine water and arrowroot in cup and add to cranberry juice, blending well. Cook until thickened, stirring constantly, about 10 minutes. Remove from heat. Stir in remaining cranberries and let cool completely. Blend in ¼ cup cassis.

About 5 to 10 minutes before serving, run sharp thin knife around inside edge of mold. Dip bottom of mold very briefly in hot water. Invert mousse onto platter. Serve immediately with cassis sauce.

Mousse can be unmolded early in day and returned to freezer.

Frozen Honey Orange Cream

8 servings

Candied Orange Peel
    Peel of 4 medium oranges, cut into very fine julienne

1 cup water
½ cup sugar
¼ teaspoon fresh lemon juice

Honey Cream
2 cups well-chilled whipping cream

2 tablespoons powdered sugar
3 tablespoons Grand Marnier

4 egg whites, room temperature
    Pinch of salt
    Pinch of cream of tartar
½ cup honey

For peel: Blanch peel in boiling water 5 minutes. Drain well; repeat.

Cook water, sugar and lemon juice in heavy medium saucepan over low heat until sugar dissolves, swirling pan occasionally. Increase heat and bring to boil. Reduce heat to simmer. Add peel and cook until softened and glazed and syrup thickens, about 35 minutes. Cool completely. Refrigerate.

For cream: Using electric mixer, beat cream with sugar in large bowl until thickened. Gradually add Grand Marnier and beat to soft peaks.

Using electric mixer with clean dry beaters, beat whites in large bowl with salt and cream of tartar until soft peaks form. Gradually add honey and beat until stiff but not dry.

Fold ¼ of whites into whipped cream to loosen. Fold in remaining whites. Spoon into pastry bag fitted with large star tip. Pipe decoratively into eight 1-cup molds. Freeze until firm, then cover and freeze until ready to serve. (*Can be prepared several days ahead.*)

Bring peel in syrup to room temperature. If cream is frozen solid, soften slightly in refrigerator. Sprinkle peel over cream. Drizzle generously with orange syrup and serve.

Biscuit Tortoni

Makes 12 to 14

½ cup crushed macaroons
½ cup almonds, toasted and crushed
¼ cup powdered sugar

2 cups whipping cream
2 tablespoons amaretto
1 tablespoon dark rum
Blanched whole almonds

Place paper liners in muffin tin. Mix macaroons, crushed almonds, sugar and 1 cup cream. Whip remaining cream and fold into macaroon mixture with amaretto and rum. Spoon into muffin cups and freeze at least 2 hours. Top each tortoni with an almond and serve.

Frozen Chocolate Chip Meringue

8 servings

3 cups whipping cream
10 ounces semisweet chocolate, coarsely chopped

4 egg whites, room temperature
⅛ teaspoon cream of tartar
Pinch of salt

⅔ cup sugar
1 teaspoon vanilla
¾ cup semisweet chocolate chips

3 tablespoons crème de cacao

Stir cream and chopped chocolate in heavy medium saucepan over medium-low heat until chocolate melts. Cool to room temperature. Press plastic wrap onto surface of chocolate cream. Refrigerate at least 4 hours.

Cut out three 7½-inch rounds of parchment. Beat whites, cream of tartar and salt until soft peaks form. Gradually add sugar and beat until stiff and shiny. Add vanilla. Gently fold in chocolate chips.

Position rack in center of oven and preheat to 200°F. Using dabs of meringue, affix parchment circles to baking sheet. Spread ¼ of meringue on each of 2 circles, smoothing to within ½ inch of edge. Spread remaining half of meringue on remaining circle, spreading to within ½ inch of edge. Bake 2 hours. Let meringues stand in turned-off oven until dry, 1 to 2 hours. Remove from baking sheet and cool completely. Remove parchment. (*Can be prepared 1 day ahead. Store in airtight container in cool dry place.*)

Using electric mixer, beat chocolate cream in large bowl until thick and soft peaks form. Fold in crème de cacao. (*Can be prepared 2 days ahead, covered and refrigerated.*) Set 1 thin meringue round on platter. Spread with half of chocolate cream. Top with other thin meringue round. Spread with remaining chocolate cream. Top with thick meringue round, pressing gently. Freeze at least 6 hours or wrap airtight and freeze up to 2 months. Let stand at room temperature 15 minutes to soften slightly before serving.

Quadruple Chocolate Suicide

8 to 10 servings

Bittersweet Chocolate Ice Cream
1³/₄ cups half and half
  2 tablespoons honey
  6 egg yolks, room temperature
  2 tablespoons sugar
  1 teaspoon vanilla
    Pinch of salt
  6 ounces extra-bittersweet or
    bittersweet chocolate, chopped
  3 tablespoons unsweetened cocoa
    powder
  2 tablespoons dark rum

Rich Chocolate Mousse
  2 cups whipping cream
  ¹/₄ cup honey
 12 egg yolks, room temperature
  ¹/₄ cup sugar
  1 teaspoon vanilla
    Pinch of salt
 12 ounces extra-bittersweet or
    bittersweet chocolate, chopped

    Shaved mint chocolate
    parfait bars*

For ice cream: Scald half and half in heavy medium saucepan. Stir in honey. Combine yolks, sugar, vanilla and salt in medium bowl. Slowly whisk in half and half. Return to pan. Stir over medium-low heat until thick enough to coat back of spoon (180°F); do not boil. Remove from heat. Add chocolate and stir until melted. Sift in cocoa, whisking to blend. Add rum. Strain into container. Cool slightly. Cover and freeze until firm, at least 8 hours. (*Ice cream can be prepared 1 day ahead.*)

    For mousse: Scald cream in heavy medium saucepan. Add honey and stir until dissolved. Combine yolks, sugar, vanilla and salt in medium bowl. Slowly whisk in cream. Return to pan. Stir over medium-low heat until thick enough to coat back of spoon (180°F); do not boil. Remove from heat. Add chocolate and stir until melted. Strain into bowl. Cool. Refrigerate until firm, at least 3 hours. (*Chocolate mousse can be prepared 1 day ahead.*)

    Place 2 scoops ice cream side by side in each dessert bowl and freeze. To serve, let ice cream soften slightly in refrigerator if frozen solid. Top each scoop of ice cream with 1 scoop of mousse. Garnish with shaved chocolate.

*A bar of layered dark chocolate and green mint chocolate. Available at most supermarkets and candy shops.

Frozen Fudge Supreme

6 servings

Walnut Meringues (makes about 16)
  ¹/₄ cup walnuts (1 ounce)
  2 large egg whites, room
    temperature
  ¹/₈ teaspoon cream of tartar
    Pinch of salt
  8 tablespoons sugar
  ¹/₂ teaspoon vanilla

Chocolate Cream
1¹/₂ cups whipping cream

  ¹/₃ cup unsweetened cocoa powder
  ¹/₄ cup sugar
    Pinch of salt

    Unsalted butter
    Sifted powdered sugar

  ¹/₂ pint (1 cup) vanilla ice cream,
    slightly softened

    Fudge Sauce*

For meringues: Position rack in center of oven and preheat to 200°F. Line baking sheet with parchment paper.

    Finely mince walnuts in processor. Using electric mixer, beat egg whites at low speed until foamy. Add cream of tartar and salt and beat at high speed until stiff but not dry. Add sugar 2 tablespoons at a time, beating until mixture is stiff. Fold in nuts and vanilla.

Spoon mixture into pastry bag fitted with No. 6 tip. Pipe onto prepared baking sheet in flat 2½-inch circles, spacing 1 inch apart. Bake 2 hours. Turn oven off, open door 3 inches and let meringues cool in oven. Gently remove meringues from paper and store in airtight container. (*Can be prepared up to 1 week ahead. Store in tightly covered container in cool, dry area.*)

For chocolate cream: Combine cream, cocoa powder, sugar and salt in jar or container with tight-fitting lid and shake well. Cover and refrigerate for at least 2 hours or overnight.

Butter six ½-cup soufflé dishes and sprinkle with sifted powdered sugar, shaking out excess.

Transfer chocolate cream to processor and blend until consistency of whipped cream, about 25 seconds. Break meringues into pieces. Add to work bowl and mix lightly using 4 on/off turns just until meringues are chopped and blended in.

Divide mixture evenly among prepared dishes. Freeze until firm, 2½ to 3 hours. Divide vanilla ice cream into 6 portions and spread evenly across top of each dish. Cover with plastic wrap. Freeze until solid, at least 3 hours.

Remove dishes from freezer 10 minutes before serving time. Dip knife in warm water and run around edge of each dish. Invert desserts onto individual plates. Drizzle 2 or more tablespoons fudge sauce around base and serve.

*Fudge Sauce

Makes about 1½ cups

⅔ cup sugar	broken into pieces
½ cup cold water	½ cup whipping cream
4 ounces unsweetened chocolate,	1 teaspoon vanilla (optional)

Combine ⅓ cup sugar with water in small saucepan. Bring to boil over high heat. Reduce heat to low and simmer 1 minute. Remove syrup from heat.

Mince chocolate with remaining ⅓ cup sugar in processor until chocolate is as fine as sugar, about 1 minute. With machine running, pour syrup through feed tube in slow, steady stream. With machine still running, add cream and vanilla and blend 30 seconds.

Frozen Chartreuse-Mint Chocolate Soufflé

8 to 10 servings

3 ounces mint chocolate, coarsely chopped	1¾ cups well-chilled whipping cream
1 ounce bittersweet or semisweet chocolate, coarsely chopped	½ cup plus 2 tablespoons green Chartreuse
1 tablespoon unsalted butter	*Mint Chocolate Soufflé*
	4 egg yolks, room temperature
1¼ teaspoons unflavored gelatin	3 tablespoons sugar
¼ cup green Chartreuse	¼ teaspoon vanilla
¼ cup crème de menthe	Pinch of salt
	2 egg whites, room temperature
Chartreuse Soufflé	Pinch of cream of tartar
9 egg yolks, room temperature	½ cup well-chilled whipping cream
½ cup sugar	¼ cup crème de menthe
¼ teaspoon vanilla	
Pinch of salt	2 ounces mint chocolate parfait* or mint chocolate
3 egg whites, room temperature	
Pinch of cream of tartar	

Wrap buttered strip of parchment around 6-cup soufflé dish, extending 4 inches above edge. Secure with string. Place in freezer while preparing soufflés.

Melt 3 ounces mint chocolate, bittersweet chocolate and butter over simmering water until smooth.

Soften 1 teaspoon gelatin in ¼ cup Chartreuse in heatproof bowl. Soften ¼ teaspoon gelatin in ¼ cup crème de menthe in another heatproof bowl. Set both bowls in pan of simmering water and stir until gelatin dissolves. Turn off heat; leave bowls in water.

For Chartreuse soufflé: Beat yolks with sugar, vanilla and salt in large bowl of electric mixer until pale yellow and slowly dissolving ribbon forms when beaters are lifted, about 6 minutes. Slowly beat in Chartreuse-gelatin mixture. Beat whites with cream of tartar in another bowl until soft peaks form. Gently fold ¼ of whites into yolks to lighten, then fold in remaining whites. Whip cream in another large bowl until just beginning to thicken. Slowly add Chartreuse, beating until soft peaks form. Gently fold cream into egg mixture. Return mixture to whipped cream bowl and refrigerate.

For mint chocolate soufflé: Beat yolks, sugar, vanilla and salt in large bowl of electric mixer until pale yellow and slowly dissolving ribbon forms when beaters are lifted, about 6 minutes. Slowly beat in crème de menthe-gelatin mixture and melted chocolate. Beat whites with cream of tartar in another bowl until soft peaks form. Gently fold ¼ of whites into yolks to lighten, then fold in remaining whites. Whip cream in another bowl until just beginning to thicken. Slowly add crème de menthe, beating until soft peaks form. Fold into egg mixture.

To assemble: Gently fold Chartreuse soufflé to recombine. Spoon ⅕ of Chartreuse soufflé into prepared dish. Carefully spoon in ¼ of mint chocolate soufflé, leaving 1-inch border. Cover completely with another ⅕ of Chartreuse soufflé. Continue layering, making 3 more mint chocolate layers, leaving 1-inch border each time, and 3 more Chartreuse layers (mint chocolate mixture should not show through). Freeze at least 12 hours.

Shave mint chocolate parfait onto waxed paper using vegetable peeler. Refrigerate until chilled. Just before serving, carefully unwrap collar from soufflé. Sprinkle top of soufflé with shaved chocolate. Serve immediately.

*A bar of layered dark chocolate and green mint chocolate. Available at most supermarkets and candy shops.

Frozen Chocolate Rum Sponge Roll with Hot Fudge Sauce

A wonderful do-ahead party dessert.

10 to 12 servings

Cocoa Cream
  3 cups well-chilled whipping cream
  ½ cup unsweetened cocoa powder
  ½ cup sugar

1½ tablespoons dark rum

Cake
  ¾ cup cake flour
  1 teaspoon baking powder
  ½ teaspooon baking soda
    Pinch of salt

  3 eggs, separated
  1 tablespoon white vinegar

  1 tablespoon water
¾ cup sugar
  3 ounces semisweet chocolate, broken into pieces
⅓ cup boiling water
  1 tablespoon dark rum
  1 teaspoon vanilla

1½ tablespoons powdered sugar

    Hot Fudge Sauce*

For cocoa cream: Combine cream, cocoa and sugar in medium bowl. Cover and refrigerate at least 1 hour.

Transfer chilled cream mixture to processor and whip until thickened, about 1 minute. Add rum and blend 3 seconds. Remove from work bowl and refrigerate until ready to use. Wash and dry work bowl.

For cake: Position rack in center of oven and preheat to 325°F. Line 11 × 17-inch jelly roll pan with waxed paper, extending 2 inches beyond edges of pan. Butter paper; dust lightly with all purpose flour, shaking off excess. Sift cake flour, baking powder, soda and salt into mixing bowl.

Place egg whites in processor work bowl and whip 8 seconds. With machine running, pour vinegar and 1 tablespoon water through feed tube and process until whites are whipped and hold their shape, about 70 seconds. Gently transfer to 1-quart mixing bowl; do not wash work bowl. Combine sugar and chocolate in work bowl and chop chocolate using 6 on/off turns, then process until chocolate is as fine as sugar, about 1 minute, stopping as necessary to scrape down sides and cover of work bowl. With machine running, pour boiling water through feed tube and blend until chocolate is melted, about 30 seconds. Scrape down work bowl. Add yolks, rum and vanilla and blend 1 minute.

Spoon sifted dry ingredients evenly onto chocolate mixture. Place egg whites atop dry ingredients. Blend using 2 on/off turns; scrape down sides of work bowl. Blend using 2 more on/off turns just until batter is mixed. (Some streaks of egg white may remain; do not overprocess. Remove steel knife and blend mixture gently with spatula if necessary.)

Spoon batter into prepared pan, spreading evenly. Tap pan lightly on counter to remove any air pockets. Bake until tester inserted in center comes out clean, about 14 to 15 minutes. Sift powdered sugar evenly over top. Cover cake with sheet of waxed paper, then with damp kitchen towel. Carefully invert cake onto waxed paper and towel, then transfer to rack(s) to cool, about 20 to 30 minutes. Peel off top sheet of waxed paper. Cover cake with sheet of foil; invert onto foil. (*Can be prepared ahead to this point and rolled up loosely in foil, waxed paper and towel until ready to assemble.*)

To assemble: Reserve 1½ cups cocoa cream for frosting roll; refrigerate. Remove towel and waxed paper from cake. Spread remaining cream evenly over cake, leaving ½-inch border on all sides. Starting with 1 short end, roll cake up as tightly as possible, using foil as aid. When completely rolled, place sheet of plastic wrap over roll and shape into even cylinder. Transfer roll to baking sheet. Discard plastic wrap. Frost cake with reserved cocoa cream. Freeze until firm, then place in large plastic bag, seal airtight and freeze.

About 2 hours before serving, remove cake from plastic bag. Transfer to platter and refrigerate. To serve, pour some of hot fudge sauce on dessert plates. Top with slice of cake. Pass remaining sauce separately.

*Hot Fudge Sauce

This thick sauce has an intense chocolate flavor and silken texture.

Makes about 1¾ cups

1¼ cups sugar
4 ounces unsweetened chocolate, broken into pieces
¼ cup (½ stick) unsalted butter, cut into 2 pieces, room temperature
½ cup milk, heated to simmer
1 tablespoon vanilla
1 teaspoon baking powder
Pinch of salt

Combine sugar and chocolate in processor and mix using 6 on/off turns, then process until chocolate is as fine as sugar, about 1 minute. Add butter and blend 1 minute. With machine running, pour hot milk through feed tube and blend until chocolate is melted, about 30 seconds, stopping as necessary to scrape down sides of work bowl. Add vanilla, baking powder and salt and blend 30 seconds. (*Can be prepared ahead to this point and chilled.*)

Transfer sauce to top of double boiler set over simmering water. Warm until sugar is completely dissolved and sauce is heated through, stirring occasionally, about 15 minutes. Serve hot.

5 🍎 Pastries, Tarts and Crepes

When dinner should conclude with something light and refreshing, a mousse, soufflé or meringue is perfect. For a balmy-weather treat nothing beats a frozen dessert. But when you want the hearty goodness of buttery-rich pastry or warm, flavorfully sauced crepes, this is the place to look.

Short crusts, puff pastry and paper-thin phyllo dough all turn up here, creating desserts of very different character. The butter-based tart crusts used in Manor House Apple Torte (page 64), Tyrolean Nuss Torte (page 67), and Sabayon Cream and Strawberry Tart (page 71) have old-fashioned charm. Puff pastry sweets such as Pomme Surprise (page 64), Strawberry Delights (page 72), and Barquette of Two Chocolates (page 73) offer the refined elegance of classic French *pâtisserie*, while Baklava (page 68) and Bourma (page 69), made with phyllo dough, are exquisite Middle Eastern specialties.

And then there are crepes, which few desserts can match for pure showmanship. Though they never fail to impress, crepes are simple to make ahead of time, usually requiring only minor assembly before serving. They lend themselves to all manner of attractive presentations. Apple Crepes with Cider Beurre Blanc (page 76) are folded into triangles and served hot; Buckwheat Crepes with Maple Ice Cream and Maple Sauce (page 77) are rolled up and served cold; for Lemon Meringue Gâteau (page 79) the crepes are stacked. And of course the selection has to include a flambé recipe—filled Apple Pancakes Flambéed with Apple Brandy (page 75). Any one of them will provide a memorable ending for a special dinner.

❦ Pastries and Tarts

Manor House Apple Torte

Use tart, flavorful, but not overly juicy apples, such as Granny Smiths.

8 to 10 servings

Crust
2½ cups all purpose flour
 1 cup (2 sticks) well-chilled
   unsalted butter, cut into 16 pieces
 ¼ cup sugar
 1 egg
 2 tablespoons cold water
 ½ teaspoon salt

Apple Filling
 2 pounds tart cooking apples,
   peeled, cored and thinly sliced

 ½ cup sugar
 ½ cup golden raisins
 ½ cup chopped toasted hazelnuts

Hazelnut Topping
 ⅓ cup unsalted butter, room
   temperature
 ⅓ cup firmly packed brown sugar
 ¼ cup chopped toasted hazelnuts

 Powdered sugar
 Whipped cream

For crust: Mix flour and butter in processor using on/off turns until mixture resembles coarse meal. Add sugar, egg, water and salt and blend until dough just starts to come together (do not form ball). Gather dough into disc. Wrap in plastic and chill 1 hour. (Dough can also be made by hand.)

Preheat oven to 400°F. Butter 10-inch springform pan. Divide dough into 2 pieces. Roll each out between waxed paper to 12-inch round, refrigerating as necessary to keep firm enough to work. Fit 1 round into prepared pan, bringing edge 1 inch up sides.

For filling: Arrange half of apples in pastry, overlapping slices. Sprinkle with half of sugar, raisins and nuts. Repeat with remaining apples, sugar, raisins and nuts. Top with second pastry round, pressing edges to seal.

For topping: Cream butter and brown sugar until smooth. Mix in nuts.

Spread topping over torte. Pierce all over with fork. Place pan on rimmed baking sheet. Bake torte until golden brown, about 45 minutes. Serve warm or at room temperature. Dust top lightly with sugar and accompany with cream.

Pomme Surprise

These fanciful apple-filled puff pastries are served with a creamy vanilla custard sauce.

Makes 8

 2 tablespoons (¼ stick) butter
 3 large apples, peeled, cored and
   thinly sliced
 ½ cup fresh orange juice
 3 tablespoons finely grated orange
   peel
 1 tablespoon orange marmalade
 1 tablespoon Grand Marnier

 1 pound well-chilled puff pastry
   (see page 74)

 Cinnamon sugar

Vanilla Custard Sauce
 2 cups milk
 ¾ cup sugar
 4 egg yolks, room temperature,
   beaten to blend
 1 teaspoon vanilla

Melt butter in heavy large skillet over medium heat. Add apples and cook until softened, stirring occasionally, about 5 minutes. Add juice, peel and marmalade and cook until almost all liquid is absorbed, stirring occasionally. Add Grand Marnier and cook until almost all liquid is absorbed.

Roll puff pastry out on lightly floured surface to thickness of ¼ inch. Cut out 8 "leaves," each 6 inches long from stem to tip and 3 inches across at widest point. Arrange on baking sheet. Using sharp knife, trace line around perimeter of each leaf about ½ inch from edge, cutting halfway through dough. Cut leaf vein design in center of each. Chill at least 15 minutes.

Preheat oven to 350°F. Sprinkle pastry with cinnamon sugar. Bake until puffed and golden, about 25 minutes.

Meanwhile, prepare sauce: Cook milk and sugar in heavy medium saucepan over low heat until sugar dissolves, swirling pan occasionally. Increase heat and bring just to boil. Whisk ¼ cup milk mixture into yolks, then whisk back into pan. Stir over medium-low heat until sauce thickens, 8 to 10 minutes; do not boil or sauce will curdle. Blend in vanilla.

Cool pastry slightly on rack. Cut through traced line and lift out top to create lid. Remove any uncooked pastry. Cover bottom of plate with sauce. Set pastry shell in center. Fill with apples. Top with lid and serve.

Baked Almond Apples in Pastry

4 servings

Pastry
- 1 cup all purpose flour
- ½ teaspoon sugar
- ½ teaspoon finely grated lemon peel
- Pinch of salt
- ½ cup (1 stick) well-chilled unsalted butter, cut into ½-inch pieces
- 2 tablespoons cold water

Apples
- ½ cup whipping cream
- ½ cup apple cider
- 2 tablespoons vanilla
- Pinch of cinnamon
- 4 small baking apples
- ½ lemon
- 2 teaspoons unsalted butter

Sauce
- Whipping cream
- 3 egg yolks, room temperature
- ⅓ cup sugar
- 1 tablespoon unsalted butter
- Freshly grated nutmeg

- 7 ounces almond paste
- 1 egg white
- Sifted powdered sugar

- ½ cup apricot preserves, melted, strained and cooled

- 1 egg, beaten to blend with 1 tablespoon water
- ½ cup apricot preserves, melted, strained and cooled (optional)

For pastry: Combine 1 cup flour, sugar, lemon peel and salt in medium bowl. Mix in butter using fingertips until mixture is consistency of fine meal. Add water and gather ingredients into a ball. Turn out onto work surface and do a *fraisage* (smear dough out along surface with heel of hand). Reform ball; repeat fraisage. Sprinkle dough with flour, wrap in plastic and chill at least 1 hour.

For apples: Preheat oven to 350°F. Mix cream, cider, vanilla and cinnamon in baking pan. Peel and core apples; rub with cut lemon to prevent discoloration. Place apples upright in pan; top each with ½ teaspoon butter. Cover with foil and bake until apples are half cooked, about 15 minutes. Transfer to plate to cool; reserve baking liquid.

For sauce: Measure baking liquid; add enough cream to make 1¼ cups. Transfer to saucepan and heat through. Place egg yolks in medium bowl. Gradually beat in sugar until yolks are lemon colored and form a slowly dissolving ribbon when beaters are lifted. Beating constantly, add warm baking liquid and cream mixture. Return to saucepan. Place over medium-low heat and stir with wooden spoon until mixture is thick enough to leave path when finger is drawn across spoon (180°F). Remove from heat and stir in butter and nutmeg. Place plastic wrap on surface of sauce to prevent skin from forming. Let cool, then refrigerate until well chilled.

Crumble almond paste onto work surface. Moisten with egg white and knead until smooth enough to roll, adding sifted powdered sugar as necessary. Divide into 4 parts. Roll each between 2 pieces of plastic wrap into 7-inch circle.

One at a time, dry apples with paper towels. Brush inside and outside with preserves. Discard top piece of plastic wrap from almond paste circle and set apple in center. Bring almond paste up around apple and pinch edges together on top. Peel off bottom piece of plastic wrap. Set apples on small platter without sides touching and refrigerate.

Grease baking sheet. Divide pastry into 4 parts, reserving small piece to form 4 pastry leaves and stems. One at a time, roll each between 2 pieces of plastic wrap into 7-inch circle. Discard top piece of plastic wrap. Using metal spatula to lift apple from platter, place an apple in center of pastry. Bring pastry up around apple and pinch edges together on top. Peel off bottom piece of plastic and set apple seam side down on baking sheet. Form leaves and stems from reserved pastry and set on apples. Chill at least 1 hour before baking.

One hour before serving, preheat oven to 425°F. Brush pastries with beaten egg and bake until well browned, about 30 minutes. Let cool 15 minutes. Transfer apples to individual plates. Pipe thin ribbon of melted preserves around base of each apple, if desired, and surround with band of chilled sauce.

Pastry can be prepared up to 5 days ahead. Apples can be baked, wrapped in almond paste and pastry and chilled up to 2 days. Sauce can be prepared 1 day ahead.

Rhapsody Torte

This rich dessert consists of a chewy coconut and raspberry filling in a crisp walnut crust.

8 to 10 servings

Walnut Crust
1⅓ cups all purpose flour
3 tablespoons sugar
11 tablespoons well-chilled unsalted butter, cut into small pieces
1 cup ground walnuts
1 extra-large egg yolk
⅔ cup seedless raspberry jam

Filling
1½ cups firmly packed light brown sugar

1 extra-large egg
1¼ cups chopped walnuts
¾ cup shredded coconut
¼ cup plus 1 tablespoon all purpose flour
½ teaspoon baking powder
Pinch of salt

For crust: Combine flour and sugar in processor. Cut in butter using on/off turns until mixture resembles coarse meal. Blend in walnuts. With machine running, add yolk through feed tube and mix until dough just comes together; do not form ball. Gather into ball. Press into bottom and ⅔ up sides of 9-inch springform pan. Spread bottom with half of jam and chill.

For filling: Preheat oven to 350°F. Using electric mixer, beat brown sugar and egg in large bowl until very thick, about 10 minutes. Mix in remaining ingredients. Pour into crust. Bake 30 minutes. Reduce oven temperature to 300°F. Continue baking until filling is set, about 25 minutes. Cool completely. Spread top with remaining jam. Cut torte into slices and serve.

Tyrolean Nuss Torte

Best if prepared one day ahead.

10 to 12 servings

Pastry
2½ cups unbleached all purpose flour
½ cup plus 2 tablespoons sugar
¾ teaspoon baking powder
   Pinch of salt
1 cup (2 sticks) well-chilled unsalted butter, cut into ½-inch pieces
1 egg
1 tablespoon dark rum
1 teaspoon vanilla

Nut-Rum Filling
2 tablespoons water
2 tablespoons dark rum
1¼ cups sugar
2 tablespoons (¼ stick) unsalted butter
1 cup whipping cream
5 ounces toasted blanched almonds (about 1 generous cup), coarsely ground
5 ounces toasted blanched hazelnuts (about 1 generous cup), coarsely ground

1 egg yolk blended with 1 teaspoon water
   Powdered sugar

For pastry: Mix flour, sugar, baking powder and salt in large bowl. Blend in butter with fingertips until mixture resembles coarse meal. Mix egg with rum and vanilla. Add to flour mixture and blend until dough holds together. Remove about ⅓ of dough and wrap in plastic; reserve for top of torte. Press about half of remaining dough into bottom of 9-inch springform pan. Roll remaining half of dough into rope about 1 inch in diameter. Coil rope around base of pan. Dust fingertips lightly with flour and press dough evenly up sides (about 2 inches high), being careful to make top edge very straight and even; dough will be thick. (If necessary, trim edges with knife.) Refrigerate pastry shell and reserved dough for top until ready to use. (*Can be prepared 1 to 2 days ahead and refrigerated, or frozen several months.*)

For filling: Generously butter medium baking dish. Combine water and rum in heavy medium saucepan over low heat. Add sugar and butter and swirl pan gently until sugar is dissolved. Increase heat to medium-high and cook until edges of syrup begin to darken. Reduce heat to low and cook until medium caramel color, swirling pan occasionally. Remove from heat and slowly stir in cream (be careful—mixture may spatter); caramel will form thick mass. Return to low heat and bring to boil, stirring to blend. Boil until thick syrup forms and mixture registers 218° to 220°F on candy thermometer, about 2 minutes. Mix in nuts. Pour mixture into prepared dish; let cool until just warm.

Position rack in center of oven and preheat to 400°F. Turn nut mixture into pastry-lined pan; smooth surface. Let reserved pastry stand at room temperature until soft enough to work with. Roll pastry to fit exactly over filling. Set pastry over top. Brush 1 inch of rim with egg yolk mixture. Using thin knife, loosen pastry on sides of pan and bring down over top (there should be about 1 inch of overlap). Press overlap gently to smooth and seal. Brush top generously with yolk mixture. Bake until top is rich brown, about 35 minutes. Cool on rack 10 minutes. Remove sides of springform. Transfer torte to platter. (*Torte can be prepared several days ahead, covered with plastic and stored at room temperature.*) Dust with powdered sugar just before serving.

Baklava (Walnut-filled Honey Pastry)

Be sure to have syrup prepared and fully cooled when the pastry emerges from the oven.

Makes about 3 dozen

2½ cups finely chopped walnuts
1½ cups finely chopped almonds
½ cup honey
1 tablespoon cinnamon
¼ teaspoon ground cloves
¼ teaspoon fresh lemon juice

26 phyllo pastry sheets
1½ cups (3 sticks) unsalted butter, melted and clarified

Cinnamon Syrup*

Generously butter 9 × 13 × 2-inch baking pan. Combine walnuts, almonds, honey, cinnamon, cloves and lemon juice in large bowl and set aside.

Preheat oven to 375°F. Remove 9 sheets of phyllo; cover remainder with waxed paper and damp towel to prevent drying. Begin lining baking pan 1 sheet at a time, generously brushing each sheet with melted butter. Sprinkle with half of nut mixture. Repeat procedure with next 9 sheets of phyllo; sprinkle with remaining nut mixture. Top with remaining 8 sheets of phyllo, generously brushing each sheet with butter. Trim edges. Brush top generously with melted butter.

Using sharp knife (preferably serrated), make 6 or 7 lengthwise cuts in baklava (depending on size of pieces desired), keeping knife straight and slicing through all layers (use your free hand to hold phyllo gently behind knife).

After all lengthwise cuts are made, slice diagonally into diamonds beginning at upper corner of pan. Brush again with melted butter.

Bake 30 minutes, basting twice with melted butter. Reduce oven temperature to 350°F and continue baking until crisp and golden, about 30 to 40 minutes. Spoon cooled syrup evenly over hot baklava. Let baklava cool completely in pan before removing pieces.

Baklava pieces can be wrapped individually in plastic and stored in airtight container in refrigerator up to 2 months.

*Cinnamon Syrup

Makes about 2¾ cups

1½ cups honey
1⅓ cups water
4 whole cloves

3 cinnamon sticks
Chopped peel of 1 lemon

Combine all ingredients in medium saucepan and bring to boil over medium-high heat. Reduce heat to medium-low and continue boiling gently for 15 to 20 minutes. Let cool completely. Strain before using.

Kadayif (Walnut- or Cheese-filled Dessert Squares)

The syrup can be made well in advance. Add a wedge of lemon to prevent crystallization and store, covered, in refrigerator.

Makes 12 to 15

1 pound kadayif dough*
¾ cup (1½ sticks) unsalted butter, melted

Filling
1½ cups chopped walnuts
1½ tablespoons sugar
1 teaspoon cinnamon
or

12 ounces Monterey Jack cheese, sliced

Syrup
2 cups sugar
1½ cups water
1 teaspoon fresh lemon juice

Preheat oven to 400°F. Pull dough apart and fluff in large bowl. Toss lightly with butter. Spread half into 9 × 12-inch baking dish.

For filling: Combine walnuts, sugar and cinnamon and sprinkle over dough, or top evenly with cheese slices. Cover with remaining dough, distributing evenly. Bake until top is golden brown, about 40 minutes.

Meanwhile, prepare syrup: Mix sugar, water and lemon juice in saucepan and bring to boil. Pour half of syrup over warm kadayif. Cut while warm.

Pass remaining syrup in pitcher for those who prefer sweeter flavor.

*Kadayif is a shredded dough that can be purchased at Armenian or Greek markets.

Bourma (Walnut-filled Pastry Rolls)

Makes about 3 dozen 4-inch pieces

3 cups finely chopped walnuts
¼ cup sugar
1 teaspoon cinnamon

1 pound phyllo pastry sheets
1 cup (2 sticks) unsalted butter, melted

½ cup (1 stick) unsalted butter, melted

Syrup
3 cups sugar
2 cups water
1 tablespoon fresh lemon juice

Combine walnuts, sugar and cinnamon in mixing bowl; set aside.

Unroll phyllo; remove 2 sheets and place on work surface (keep remainder covered with waxed paper and damp towel to prevent drying). Brush top sheet lightly with some of the 1 cup melted butter. Sprinkle about 4 tablespoons nut mixture over lengthwise half of phyllo.

Use wooden dowel about ¾ inch in diameter and at least 24 inches long and place along nut-filled side of phyllo. Roll phyllo loosely around dowel. Lay dough seam side down on work surface. Lift one end of dowel and, using hands, gently push dough together from each end to form crinkled roll about 10 to 12 inches long. Slide dough off dowel. Insert index finger in each end of bourma to transfer to ungreased 11 × 17-inch jelly roll pan, or slide off dowel directly onto pan. Let stand uncovered so phyllo dries slightly while making remaining bourma.

Preheat oven to 300°F. When bourma have dried slightly, pull ends out accordion-fashion until they touch 11-inch edges of pan. Pour remaining ½ cup butter over top and bake until lightly browned, about 35 to 40 minutes.

For syrup, combine sugar, water and lemon juice in saucepan and boil until slightly thickened. Keep warm.

Drain excess butter from jelly roll pan. Using serrated knife, immediately cut pastries into pieces about 4 inches long. Pour warm syrup over warm pastries. Serve at room temperature.

Chewton Glen's Caramelized Pears with Pear Sabayon

6 servings

Rich Butter Pastries
9 tablespoons well-chilled unsalted butter, cut into 9 pieces
4½ tablespoons cold water
1½ tablespoons sugar
¼ teaspoon salt
¾ cup plus 2 tablespoons all purpose flour

Caramelized Pears
3 8-ounce ripe but firm Bartlett or Anjou pears, peeled, halved and cored
1½ tablespoons unsalted butter, melted
3 tablespoons pear brandy
2 tablespoons firmly packed light brown sugar

Pear Sabayon*

For pastries: Chop butter in processor using 6 on/off turns. Add water, sugar and salt. Process 5 seconds. Add flour and process just until dough begins to gather together, about 3 seconds; do not form ball. Transfer to plastic bag. Working through bag, press dough into disc. Refrigerate at least 2 hours.

Butter 2 baking sheets. Divide dough in half. Roll 1 piece out on lightly floured surface to thickness of ¹⁄₁₆ inch. Cut out three 4½-inch circles. Transfer to prepared sheets. Repeat with remaining dough. Cover pastries and refrigerate at least 1 hour.

Position rack in center of oven and preheat to 425°F. Pierce pastries all over with fork. Bake until light brown, 6 to 7 minutes. Cool completely on racks. (*Can be prepared 2 days ahead and stored at room temperature or 1 month ahead and frozen. Bring pastries to room temperature before using.*)

For pears: Position rack in center of oven and preheat to 350°F. Arrange pears cut side down in baking dish. Brush with butter and 1 tablespoon brandy. Bake until beginning to soften, brushing occasionally with some of remaining brandy, 20 to 30 minutes. Brush pears with any remaining brandy and cool.

Preheat broiler. Cut each pear crosswise into ⅛-inch-thick slices, retaining pear shape. Gently press 1 teaspoon brown sugar onto each pear half. Broil 6 inches from heat until sugar caramelizes; watch carefully.

Place pears in cold oven. Turn heat to 350°F. Bake 8 minutes. Arrange pastries on another baking sheet and place in oven. Bake until pears and pastries are heated through, about 4 more minutes. Spread 3 tablespoons pear sabayon over each plate. Arrange pears atop pastries, using spatula. Fan slices slightly. Place pastries in center of plates and serve immediately.

*Pear Sabayon

Makes about 1⅓ cups

6 egg yolks
¼ cup sugar

2 tablespoons hot water
2 tablespoons pear brandy

Blend yolks, sugar, water and brandy in processor 1 minute, stopping once to scrape down sides of work bowl. Transfer mixture to top of double boiler set over simmering water. Whisk until foamy and heated through, about 6 minutes. Serve immediately.

Sabayon Cream and Strawberry Tart

8 servings

Almond Short Crust

6 tablespoons (¾ stick) unsalted butter, room temperature
2 tablespoons sugar
1 egg yolk
1 teaspoon grated lemon peel
½ teaspoon vanilla
3 drops almond extract
Pinch of salt
¾ cup plus 2 tablespoons all purpose flour
¼ cup very finely chopped blanched almonds (about ½ cup slivered)

Strawberry Glaze

½ cup strawberry jam
1½ tablespoons water
1 tablespoon orange, strawberry or black raspberry liqueur

Crème Sabayon

½ rounded teaspoon unflavored gelatin
½ cup Chardonnay
¼ cup sugar
2 egg yolks, room temperature
Pinch of salt

⅓ cup whipping cream, room temperature
1 tablespoon orange liqueur

40 large strawberries (about 1 quart)

For crust: Cream butter, sugar, egg yolk, lemon peel, vanilla, almond extract and salt in large bowl. Add flour and almonds and mix until smooth. If dough seems very sticky, refrigerate 30 minutes before using. Press crust evenly into 9-inch tart pan with removable bottom, dusting hands with flour as necessary. Refrigerate at least 1 hour or overnight, or freeze.

Preheat oven to 375°F. Bake pastry shell until brown, 20 to 25 minutes (pierce pastry once with knife tip if air bubble forms during first 10 minutes of baking). Cool completely.

For glaze: Melt jam with water in small saucepan over medium heat. Strain. Blend in liqueur and set aside.

For sabayon: Sprinkle gelatin over wine in large metal bowl and let stand several minutes until softened. Whisk in sugar, yolks and salt using circular motion until top is foamy. Place bowl over large saucepan of hot water set over low heat and continue whisking until egg mixture is thick and foamy and instant-reading thermometer registers 160°F to 165°F, about 15 minutes. Cool to room temperature, about 5 minutes, whisking occasionally.

Meanwhile, brush surface of pastry shell with strawberry glaze. Whip cream in large bowl to soft peaks. Stir liqueur into cooled sabayon. Gently fold cream into sabayon. Pour sabayon into pastry shell. Refrigerate 20 minutes or up to several hours.

Halve strawberries vertically. Arrange berries on sabayon in concentric circles cut side down and pointed side outward, overlapping slightly and using largest berries for outer circles. Brush glaze carefully over berries; do not let glaze drip on filling. (*Can be garnished up to 1 hour ahead.*) Refrigerate. Let stand at room temperature for about 10 minutes before serving.

Strawberry Delights

Makes 8

Puff Pastry
1½ cups all purpose flour
½ cup cake flour
½ teaspoon salt
 1 cup (2 sticks) well-chilled
  unsalted butter
½ cup water

Strawberries
 2 cups very small strawberries
  (or halved, if large)
⅓ cup sugar
 1 teaspoon raspberry liqueur

Pastry Cream
⅓ cup sugar
1½ tablespoons all purpose flour,
  sifted
1½ tablespoons cornstarch, sifted
 1 cup milk
 2 egg yolks, beaten to blend

¼ cup (½ stick) unsalted butter,
  room temperature
 1 tablespoon raspberry liqueur

Strawberry Coulis
½ cup sugar
½ cup water
1½ cups fresh strawberry puree
 1 tablespoon raspberry liqueur
 1 teaspoon fresh lemon juice

Cream Cheese Topping
½ cup whipping cream
 4 ounces cream cheese
 2 tablespoons sugar
  Few drops of raspberry liqueur

 1 egg yolk blended with
  ½ tablespoon water (glaze)

½ cup red currant jelly, melted

For pastry: Combine flours and salt in bowl. Set ¼ cup of mixture aside. Cut 4 tablespoons butter into remainder until mixture resembles coarse meal. Mound on surface; make large well in center. Add water to well. With one hand, quickly incorporate flour into water; do not overwork. Gather dough into rough mass. Cut through mass several times with pastry cutter until dough just starts to bind together. Wrap in plastic; chill 30 minutes.

Knead remaining ¾ cup butter and reserved ¼ cup flour mixture until same consistency as dough. Shape into 5-inch round and wrap in waxed paper. Refrigerate 30 minutes.

Roll dough out on lightly floured surface into 12-inch circle. Place butter in center of dough. Fold dough over to encase butter completely. Turn dough over. Roll package out gently and evenly into 8 × 18-inch rectangle; do not roll over edges. Fold dough over into 3 equal sections as for business letter. Press edges down lightly with rolling pin to seal. (This is 1 turn.)

Give dough a quarter turn so it opens like a book. Roll again into 8 × 18-inch rectangle. Fold into thirds. (This is second turn.) Wrap in waxed paper, then plastic, and refrigerate at least 1 hour. Give dough 2 more turns; refrigerate at least 2 hours or overnight. Give dough last 2 turns (for total of 6) and refrigerate at least 2 hours before rolling and cutting. (*Can be prepared up to 3 days ahead, wrapped and refrigerated.*)

Roll dough out on lightly floured surface into square ½ to ¾ inch thick. Set on baking sheet and freeze 20 minutes. Trim sides of dough. Cut into 4 strips about 4 inches wide. Freeze until firm. Cut each strip into two 4-inch squares. Freeze at least 30 minutes.

For strawberries: Mix berries, sugar and liqueur. Chill at least 1 hour.

For pastry cream: Combine sugar, flour and cornstarch in medium bowl. Bring milk to rolling boil. Whisk half of milk into sugar mixture. Whisk in yolks until smooth. Reboil remaining milk. Whisk sugar mixture into milk until very thick, about 30 seconds. Remove from heat and whisk until cool. Whisk in butter 1 tablespoon at a time. Blend in liqueur. Cover with plastic and refrigerate until ready to use. (*Can be prepared up to 1 day ahead.*)

For coulis: Cook sugar and water in heavy small saucepan over low heat until sugar dissolves, swirling pan occasionally. Increase heat and boil 4 minutes or until candy thermometer registers 200°F. Cool. Drain liquid from whole strawberries into heavy small saucepan. Boil until candy thermometer registers 200°F. Blend strawberry syrup into strawberry puree. Add sugar syrup to puree to desired sweetness (oversweeten; coulis will lose sweetness after refrigeration). Blend in liqueur and lemon juice. Refrigerate until ready to use. (*Can be prepared up to 1 day ahead, covered and refrigerated.*)

For topping: Gradually beat cream into cream cheese in bowl of heavy-duty mixer at medium speed until semifirm, about 10 minutes. Blend in sugar and liqueur. Refrigerate until ready to use. (*Can be prepared up to 1 day ahead.*)

Preheat oven to 425°F. Brush egg glaze over pastry squares. Arrange on large baking sheet. Bake 20 minutes (if tops brown too quickly, cover loosely with foil). Split each square in half horizontally. Return to oven cut side up and bake until insides are dry, 3 minutes.

To assemble: Fill 8 halves with pastry cream. Cover with remaining 8 halves. Brush tops lightly with melted currant jelly. Arrange whole strawberries over. Brush strawberries with jelly to glaze.

Spoon 3 tablespoons strawberry coulis into each of 8 dessert plates. Place pastry in center. Quarter any remaining whole strawberries and arrange around pastry in coulis. Pass cream cheese topping separately.

Barquette of Two Chocolates

An impressive finale. Although the dessert should be assembled the same day it is served, everything but the sauce can be made one day ahead.

10 to 12 servings

White Chocolate Filling
15 ounces white chocolate, chopped
3/4 cup plus 2 tablespoons whipping cream
1 cup (2 sticks) unsalted butter, room temperature

Dark Chocolate Filling
1/2 cup sugar
1/4 cup water
1 tablespoon fresh lemon juice
5 egg yolks, room temperature

1 cup (2 sticks) unsalted butter, room temperature
18 ounces extra-bittersweet or bittersweet chocolate, melted and cooled

Pastry
2 cups sugar
3 pounds Puff Pastry (see following recipe)

Riesling Sauce*

For white chocolate: Melt chocolate with cream in double boiler over barely simmering water, stirring until smooth. Cool to room temperature. Whisk in butter. Transfer to medium bowl and set in larger bowl filled with ice water. Stir until thick enough to spread. (*Can be prepared 1 day ahead and refrigerated. Let filling stand at room temperature until it is spreadable but still thick, stirring occasionally.*)

For dark chocolate: Heat sugar, water and lemon juice in heavy small saucepan over low heat, swirling pan occasionally, until sugar dissolves. Increase heat and boil until candy thermometer registers 230°F (thread stage). Remove from heat. Beat yolks with electric mixer until pale yellow. Slowly beat in hot syrup; continue beating until mixture is cool. Beat butter in medium bowl until light and fluffy. Beat in half of yolks, then chocolate, then remaining yolks. Set into large bowl filled with ice water and stir until thick enough to spread. (*Can be prepared 1 day ahead and refrigerated. Let stand at room temperature until spreadable but still thick, stirring occasionally.*)

For pastry: Position rack in lower third of oven and preheat to 400°F. Butter heavy 10 × 15-inch baking sheet (preferably nonstick). Butter underside of another heavy 10 × 15-inch baking sheet. Sprinkle work surface generously with sugar. Cut pastry into 3 pieces. Wrap 2 pieces and refrigerate. Roll 1 piece of dough out on sugar to ¼-inch-thick rectangle, turning occasionally and adding more sugar if dough sticks. Transfer to buttered sheet, brushing off excess sugar. Top with second sheet, buttered side resting on pastry. Place heavy roasting pan or skillet on top. Bake 10 minutes. Reduce heat to 375°F and continue baking until sugar caramelizes, watching carefully to prevent burning, about 20 minutes. Transfer pastry to rack. Increase heat to 400°F. Repeat with remaining pastry. Cool completely.

Using serrated knife, cut pastry into eight 4½ × 11½-inch rectangles.

To assemble: Place 1 pastry layer on platter. Spread evenly to edges with ⅓ of white chocolate filling. Top with another pastry layer, pressing gently into filling to secure. Refrigerate 5 minutes to firm. Spread evenly to edges with ⅓ of dark chocolate filling. Top with another pastry layer, pressing gently to secure. Refrigerate 5 minutes. Continue layering, ending with pastry (only 7 pastry rectangles will be used); chill bowls of fillings slightly if fillings soften. Cover barquette and refrigerate until firm, about 30 minutes. (*Can be prepared up to 3 hours ahead.*)

Cut chilled barquette crosswise into ½-inch-thick slices, using serrated knife dipped in hot water and wiped dry. Arrange on plates. Let stand at room temperature 15 minutes. Spoon sauce around pastry and serve.

*Riesling Sauce

Makes about 4 cups

1½ cups dry Riesling	8 egg yolks, room temperature
24 dried cassia buds (available at Chinese markets), optional	¾ cup plus 2 tablespoons sugar
2 3-inch cinnamon sticks	1 teaspoon vanilla
6 whole cloves	Pinch of salt
	½ cup kirsch

Bring first 4 ingredients to simmer in medium saucepan. Cool to room temperature. Bring to simmer again. Strain wine into measuring cup.

Beat yolks, sugar, vanilla and salt in top of double boiler with electric mixer until pale yellow and slowly dissolving ribbon forms when beaters are lifted. Place over simmering water. Slowly add wine, then kirsch, whisking until mixture triples in volume, about 10 minutes. Serve immediately.

Puff Pastry

Makes about 3 pounds

6 cups sifted all purpose flour	1 cup (about) ice water
¾ teaspoon salt	
3 cups (6 sticks) chilled unsalted butter, cut into ½-inch pieces	

Combine flour and salt in mound on work surface. Mix in butter until well coated. Make long well down center of flour. Add ¼ cup water to well. With fingertips extended and palms turned upward, mix water into flour by tossing gently. Repeat, adding water ¼ cup at a time until dough just holds together. Flatten into rectangle. Wrap in plastic and refrigerate 20 minutes.

Gently roll dough out on lightly floured surface to 10 × 24-inch rectangle. (If at any time dough contracts and is hard to roll, refrigerate 30 minutes.) Brush off excess flour. Fold dough over into 3 equal sections as for business letter. (This is 1 turn.) Give dough quarter turn so it opens like a book. Roll again into 10 × 24-inch rectangle. Fold in thirds. (This is second turn.) Wrap pastry in plastic and refrigerate for at least 20 minutes.

Repeat for 2 more turns; refrigerate dough at least 20 minutes or overnight. Repeat twice again (for total of 6 turns). Refrigerate at least 20 minutes before rolling and cutting. (*Can be prepared 3 days ahead.*)

 Crepes

Apple Pancakes Flambéed with Apple Brandy

8 servings

Crepes
- 1 cup all purpose flour
- 2 eggs, room temperature
- 1/2 teaspoon vanilla
  Pinch of salt
- 1 cup milk

Apple Compote
- 1 3/4 pounds Golden Delicious apples, peeled, cored and thinly sliced
- 1/4 cup sugar
- 1 tablespoon water

- 3 tablespoons butter
- 3 tablespoons Calvados or kirsch

Milk (if necessary)
- 1 tablespoon finely chopped candied orange peel
- 1/2 teaspoon minced fresh mint

- 1/4 cup sugar
- 1 tablespoon fresh lemon juice
- 1/2 cup fresh orange juice
  Vanilla ice cream (optional)

For crepes: Sift flour into medium bowl. Make well in center. Add eggs, vanilla and salt to well and whisk to blend. Gradually incorporate flour, whisking until smooth. Add 1 cup milk in slow steady stream, whisking until smooth. Let batter stand 1 hour.

For compote: Heat apples, 1/4 cup sugar and water in heavy medium saucepan over low heat, swirling pan occasionally, until sugar dissolves. Increase heat and simmer until chunky applesauce forms, stirring frequently, about 15 minutes.

Melt butter in crepe pan. Cool slightly. Stir 1 tablespoon into crepe batter. Pour remaining butter into small cup; skim off foam to clarify. Add 1 tablespoon Calvados to batter.

Heat crepe pan over medium-high heat. Brush lightly with clarified butter. Remove pan from heat. Working quickly, ladle about 2 tablespoons batter into corner of pan, tilting so batter just coats bottom. Return excess to bowl. Cook crepe until bottom is brown, loosening edges with knife. Turn crepe over and cook second side until speckled brown. Slide onto plate. Repeat with remaining batter, stirring batter before making each crepe and greasing pan as necessary. (Thin batter with milk if too thick.)

Add 1 tablespoon Calvados, orange peel and mint to apples. Boil until mixture mounds in spoon, stirring constantly, about 2 minutes. Spread 2 1/2 tablespoons apple mixture on each crepe. Roll up as for jelly roll.

Heat 1/4 cup sugar in heavy large skillet over low heat, swirling pan occasionally, until sugar dissolves. Increase heat and boil until light caramel color.

Stir in lemon juice, then orange juice. Bring to boil, stirring constantly. Reduce heat to low. Add pancakes to skillet seam side down and heat. Pour remaining 1 tablespoon Calvados into corner of pan and ignite with match. When flames subside, transfer pancakes to warm platter. Cover with syrup. Top with vanilla ice cream if desired and serve immediately.

Apple Crepes with Cider Beurre Blanc

6 servings

Crepes (makes 24 6½-inch crepes)
1 cup all purpose flour
1½ cups milk, room temperature
¼ cup water
¼ cup Calvados
3 eggs, room temperature
2 egg yolks, room temperature
2 tablespoons sugar
⅛ teaspoon freshly ground cardamon
⅛ teaspoon freshly grated nutmeg
⅛ teaspoon cinnamon

¼ cup (½ stick) unsalted butter

Caramel Apple Filling
12 medium cooking apples, preferably Pippin or Greening (about 3 pounds)

1 to 2 tablespoons fresh lemon juice

2 cups sugar
1 cup water
6 whole walnuts, toasted

¼ cup (½ stick) unsalted butter, cut into small pieces
¼ cup sugar or to taste

2 tablespoons (¼ stick) unsalted butter, melted
Cider Beurre Blanc*

For crepes: Place flour in medium bowl. Whisk in about ⅔ cup milk a little at a time to make smooth paste. Gradually whisk in remaining milk with water, Calvados, eggs and yolks. Stir in sugar, cardamom, nutmeg and cinnamon. Strain batter if any lumps remain. Cover and let stand at room temperature for 1 hour.

Melt butter in crepe pan or 6- to 7-inch skillet. Let cool, then mix 2 tablespoons into batter. Pour remaining butter into small cup and spoon off foam.

Heat crepe pan over medium-high heat. Brush with some of melted butter and heat until almost smoking. Remove pan from heat. Ladle about 3 to 4 tablespoons batter into corner of pan, then tilt pan until bottom is covered with thin layer of batter; pour out any excess.

Return pan to medium-high heat, loosen edges of crepe with knife tip and cook until bottom of crepe is browned, about 1 minute, shaking pan in circle to prevent sticking. Turn crepe and cook another minute until second side is browned. Slide crepe out onto plate. Repeat with remaining batter, stacking crepes on top of each other. Let cool completely. Cover with plastic wrap and refrigerate. (*Freeze crepes if they will be kept more than 4 days.*)

For filling: Peel, quarter and core apples. Cut into slices ¼ inch thick and transfer to bowl. Toss with lemon juice.

Preheat oven to 400°F; grease small plate. Combine sugar and water in small saucepan and cook over low heat, swirling pan occasionally, until sugar is dissolved. Increase heat and cook until syrup is light brown, washing down any crystals clinging to sides of pan using brush dipped in cold water. Remove from heat. Using trussing needle, quickly dip walnuts one at a time into caramel, then push off onto greased plate. Return caramel to very low heat just long enough to remelt, then pour into 9 × 12-inch gratin pan, tilting pan so caramel covers bottom evenly.

Sprinkle apples over caramel. Dot with pieces of butter. Cover with buttered parchment paper buttered side down. Bake, stirring occasionally with wooden spoon, until apples are tender when pierced with knife, about 25 minutes. Taste and add sugar if needed. Let apples cool completely, stirring occasionally.

To assemble: Butter large shallow baking pans. Spread crepes with apples and baking juices. Fold into triangles and arrange in single layer in pans. Cover with foil until serving time.

Preheat oven to 400°F. Drizzle melted butter over crepes. Re-cover with foil and bake until heated through, about 5 minutes. Spoon cider beurre blanc into center of 6 heated dinner plates. Arrange 4 crepes with tips toward center on each. Place caramelized walnut in middle and serve immediately.

Crepes can be filled up to 1 day ahead. Bring to room temperature before drizzling with butter and baking.

*Cider Beurre Blanc

Makes about 1 cup

1 cup cider, preferably hard
¼ cup cider vinegar
1 teaspoon vanilla
Pinch of cinnamon

2 tablespoons sugar
1 cup (2 sticks) well-chilled unsalted butter, cut into 16 pieces

Combine cider, vinegar, vanilla and cinnamon in heavy small saucepan and bring to boil. Let boil until reduced to about 2 tablespoons, about 20 minutes. Reduce heat to low, add sugar and cook, swirling pan occasionally, until sugar is dissolved. Remove from heat and whisk in 2 pieces of butter. Return to low heat and whisk in remaining butter 2 pieces at a time. (*Mixture should be creamy; if at any time butter is melting rather than thickening sauce, remove from heat before adding more butter.*) Serve hot.

Buckwheat Crepes with Maple Ice Cream and Maple Sauce

6 to 8 servings

Ice Cream
1 cup pure maple syrup
4 egg yolks
2 tablespoons coffee liqueur
1 teaspoon vanilla

3 cups well-chilled whipping cream

Crepes
½ cup all purpose flour
½ cup buckwheat flour*
2 tablespoons sugar
¼ teaspoon salt

4 eggs
¾ cup milk
½ cup (about) water

6 tablespoons (¾ stick) unsalted butter

Sauce
1 cup pure maple syrup
½ cup whipping cream

Strawberries (optional garnish)

For ice cream: Bring syrup to boil in heavy large saucepan. Beat yolks in large bowl until thick. Slowly beat in hot syrup. Return to saucepan and stir over medium-low heat with wooden spatula until custard thickens enough to leave path on back of spatula when finger is drawn across, about 5 minutes; *do not boil or mixture will curdle.* Pour mixture through fine sieve into large bowl. Stir in liqueur and vanilla. Cool, then refrigerate until well chilled (preferably overnight).

Beat cream almost to firm peaks. Gently fold ¼ into custard, then fold custard into remaining cream. Transfer to ice cream maker and process according to manufacturer's instructions. Turn into container and freeze several hours to mellow.

For crepes: Combine flours, sugar and salt in large bowl. Make well in center. Add eggs and ¼ cup milk to well and whisk, slowly incorporating flour, until mixture is smooth and shiny. Gradually whisk in remaining ½ cup milk. Whisk in enough water to thin batter to texture of whipping cream. (Strain batter if lumpy.) Let stand at room temperature 1 hour. (*Can be prepared 2 days ahead to this point and refrigerated.*)

Melt 6 tablespoons butter in 8-inch crepe pan or heavy skillet over medium-low heat. Mix 3 tablespoons into crepe batter. Pour remaining butter into small bowl. Warm pan over medium-high heat until hot. Remove from heat. Working quickly, ladle about 3 tablespoons batter into pan, tilting until bottom is covered with thin layer. Pour any excess batter back into bowl. Cook crepe until bottom is lightly browned, loosening edges with knife. Turn crepe over and cook second side. Slide onto plate. Repeat with remaining batter, buttering pan as necessary to prevent sticking.

For sauce: Boil syrup in heavy small saucepan over medium-high heat until candy thermometer registers 234°F (soft-ball stage). Remove from heat and stir in cream (be careful; mixture may spatter). Return to medium-high heat and stir until smooth. (*Sauce can be prepared 2 days ahead and rewarmed.*)

Just before serving, spoon ½ cup ice cream down center of each crepe and roll up cigar fashion. Arrange 1 or 2 on each plate. Top with warm sauce. Garnish with strawberries if desired.

*Available at natural foods stores.

Hungarian Cheese-filled Palacsinta

A quick dessert that shows off these renowned Hungarian pancakes to good advantage.

Makes 10 to 14

1 pint (2 cups) large-curd cream-style cottage cheese, room temperature
3 eggs, beaten
5 tablespoons sugar
1 tablespoon finely grated lemon peel
½ teaspoon cinnamon (or more to taste)
⅛ teaspoon salt
½ cup golden raisins
10 to 14 Basic Palacsinta Shells*

Topping
2 cups sour cream
2 tablespoons sugar
1 egg yolk

Preheat oven to 300°F. Butter large shallow baking dish. Press cottage cheese through fine sieve or strainer into large bowl. Beat in eggs, sugar, lemon peel, cinnamon and salt. Fold in raisins. Divide among *palacsintas*. Roll up cigar fashion and arrange seam side down in baking dish.

For topping: Combine sour cream and sugar in mixing bowl. Add yolk and blend well. Spread along top of each pancake. Bake until heated through, about 15 minutes. Serve immediately.

*Basic Palacsinta Shells

A creation of Paulette Fono, co-owner with her husband, Laszlo, of the Paprikás Fono restaurant in San Francisco.

Makes 10 to 14

3 eggs
1 cup all purpose flour
⅛ teaspoon salt
1 cup milk
½ cup club soda

Vegetable oil or butter

Beat eggs in blender on low speed about 10 seconds. Add ½ cup flour with salt and mix again. Add remaining flour with milk and blend well. Transfer to mixing bowl and add soda (*batter should be consistency of whipping cream*).

Heat 7- to 8-inch skillet over medium-high heat until hot enough that a few drops of water will "dance" on surface. Coat skillet lightly with oil or butter. Add enough batter to cover bottom of pan evenly. Cook until edges of pancake are lightly browned, about 1 minute. Turn and cook other side for 30 seconds. Turn out onto plate and cover with sheet of waxed paper. Repeat with remaining batter, coating pan with oil or butter before cooking each pancake and stirring through batter before adding to pan. Stack *palacsinta* between sheets of waxed paper.

Lemon Meringue Gâteau of Crepes

8 servings

Crepes *(makes fifteen 6-inch crepes)*
- 2 eggs
- 1 cup milk
- 2/3 cup all purpose flour
- 4 1/2 teaspoons melted butter
- 1 teaspoon sugar
- Pinch of salt

  Melted clarified butter or vegetable oil

Lemon Filling
- 4 egg yolks
- 1/2 cup sugar
- 3 tablespoons fresh lemon juice
- 3 tablespoons grated lemon peel
- 3/4 cup whipping cream, whipped

Raspberry Sauce
- 1 10-ounce package frozen raspberries, thawed and drained
- 1/4 cup sugar
- 4 1/2 teaspoons kirsch

Meringue
- 1 cup sugar
- 6 tablespoons water
- 1/4 teaspoon cream of tartar

- 2 egg whites
- 1 teaspoon orange liqueur

For crepes: Combine eggs and milk in medium bowl and blend well. Add flour, melted butter, sugar and salt and beat until smooth and shiny. Cover batter and let stand 2 hours.

Heat 6-inch crepe pan or skillet over medium heat until drop of water sizzles when dropped in pan. Remove from heat and lightly brush with melted butter or oil. Working quickly, add 2 tablespoons batter to one edge of pan, tilting and swirling until bottom is covered with thin layer of batter. Return pan to medium-high heat and cook crepe until bottom is brown, about 35 seconds. Turn (or flip) crepe over and cook on second side until lightly browned. Slide out onto plate. Top with sheet of waxed paper. Repeat with remaining batter, stirring occasionally, adjusting heat and brushing pan with more butter as necessary.

Cool crepes. Wrap in plastic and refrigerate (or freeze) if preparing ahead.

For filling: Beat yolks in top of double boiler until thick and creamy. Add sugar and mix thoroughly. Stir in lemon juice and peel. Place over simmering water and cook, stirring constantly, until mixture thickens, about 3 to 5 minutes. Pour into medium bowl. Cool completely (do not chill). Gently fold in whipped cream. Refrigerate until ready to fill crepes.

For sauce: Combine raspberries, sugar and kirsch in processor or blender and puree. Gently press through fine sieve to remove seeds. Cover and refrigerate.

For meringue: Combine sugar, water and cream of tartar in heavy small saucepan and bring to boil over medium heat, shaking pan gently until sugar is dissolved. Reduce heat, cover and simmer 3 minutes. Remove cover, increase heat to medium-high and cook, without stirring, until syrup reaches 238°F on candy thermometer (soft-ball stage). Remove from heat.

Beat egg whites in large bowl until stiff and glossy. Very slowly beat syrup into whites with mixer on medium speed. When all syrup has been added, continue beating until meringue has cooled to room temperature, about 8 to 10 minutes. Beat in orange liqueur. Cover and refrigerate 1 hour.

To assemble: Spread lemon filling evenly over 11 crepes and stack on serving platter, filling side up. Top with plain crepe. Cover with inverted bowl and refrigerate for 1 hour.

Fifteen minutes before serving, remove bowl. Swirl meringue over top and sides of crepes. Slice with serrated knife to serve. Nap with sauce.

Orange Crepes Comme Chez Soi

These wonderful yeast crepes are a bit thicker than the standard ones. The batter should be made one day ahead.

6 servings

2 large navel oranges

¾ cup fresh orange juice

6 tablespoons orange liqueur

4½ tablespoons sugar

10 tablespoons (1¼ sticks) unsalted butter, cut into 10 pieces

12 Belgian Crepes*

2 tablespoons powdered sugar

Using zester, remove peel from 1 orange (orange part only) in long thin strips (or use small sharp knife and cut julienne). Remove peel from remaining orange and white pith from both oranges and discard. Cut between membranes of oranges with small sharp knife to release segments. Reserve 12 segments for crepes.

Combine orange peel, juice, liqueur and 4½ tablespoons sugar in heavy 12-inch skillet. Simmer 3 minutes. Reduce heat to low. Whisk in unsalted butter 1 piece at a time. Set aside.

Place 1 orange segment on lower half of each crepe and fold crepe in half. Arrange in skillet with sauce, overlapping if necessary. Sift powdered sugar over. Cook over low heat 4 minutes. Carefully turn crepes, using spatula. Continue cooking until heated through, about 3 minutes. Serve hot.

*Belgian Crepes

Makes about 22

1 cup milk

2 tablespoons sugar

1 envelope dry yeast

1½ cups unbleached all purpose flour

4 eggs

1 tablespoon grated orange peel

Pinch of salt

Unsalted butter, melted

Heat milk to lukewarm (105°F to 115°F) in small saucepan. Remove from heat. Sprinkle sugar and yeast over milk and stir to dissolve. Let stand until foamy, about 10 minutes.

Combine flour, eggs, orange peel and salt in processor work bowl. With machine running, pour yeast mixture through feed tube and blend 30 seconds. Transfer to 1½-quart bowl. Cover and refrigerate overnight.

Heat 6-inch crepe pan or heavy skillet over medium-high heat. Ladle 2 tablespoons batter into corner. Tilt pan and spread batter with spatula to cover bottom of pan. Cook crepe until bottom is light golden brown. Turn crepe and cook until second side is light golden brown. Transfer to plate. Repeat with remaining batter, placing sheets of parchment between cooked crepes. (*Can be prepared ahead and refrigerated 3 days or frozen 1 month. Bring to room temperature before using.*)

6 ❦ Cakes, Tortes and Cheesecakes

This final chapter is also the longest, and with good reason: Fancy cakes and tortes are *the* special occasion dessert. You won't find any simple loaf cakes or one-bowl shortcuts here. These are, in a word, extravaganzas, adorned in every imaginable way—with custard, meringue layers, mousse fillings, pastry cream, glazes, frostings, fruit.

This is not to say the recipes are difficult. Most have multiple preparation steps, but virtually all can be tackled well in advance of serving. Even super-spectaculars like the Praline Jewel Box with Fresh Berries (page 83), Lemon Mirror Cake (page 87), Danish Othello Cake (page 90), and Derby Dacquoise Cake (page 101) pose no special problems; just take them a step at a time and you are assured of success.

One recipe, Spiced Chocolate Torte Wrapped in Chocolate Ribbons (page 103 and cover photograph), deserves particular mention. Soon after it appeared in *Bon Appétit* reader letters started pouring in, many accompanied with "documentary" snapshots and every one recounting a triumph. Most of the writers confessed to some initial skepticism—after all, rolling out chocolate in a pasta machine *is* an unorthodox technique—but all were thrilled with their fabulous results.

The cheesecake selection here is also worthy of special note. We are all cheesecake-crazy, and by now every cook has a favorite basic recipe or two. This assortment includes quite a few variations with an international flair—for example, Irish Coffee (page 107), Black Forest (page 106), Spumoni (page 115), Baklava (page 105), and Linzertorte (page 110). There is even a Chinese-inspired Eight Treasure Cheesecake (page 108), a novel and stylish finale to an oriental feast.

Cakes and Tortes

Coffee Cream Cake

12 to 14 servings

Génoise
- 3 eggs, room temperature
- 2 egg yolks, room temperature
- ½ cup sugar
- 1 teaspoon vanilla
- ⅔ cup all purpose flour, sifted

- ¼ cup (½ stick) unsalted butter, melted
- Powdered sugar

Coffee Cream
- 2 egg whites

- ½ cup sugar
- ¼ cup water

- 1 teaspoon instant coffee powder (or instant coffee crystals crushed to powder)

- 1 cup whipping cream
- ½ teaspoon vanilla

- Candy coffee beans (optional)

Position rack in lower third of oven and preheat to 350°F. Grease and flour 10 × 15-inch baking pan. Line with parchment or waxed paper cut long enough to extend over edges. Butter and flour paper, shaking off excess.

For génoise: Combine eggs, yolks and sugar in large bowl and blend well. Set bowl over warm water and continue mixing until warmed through. Remove from heat and beat at medium speed of electric mixer until tripled in volume. Beat in vanilla. Fold in flour in 2 or 3 additions.

Fold small amount of batter into melted butter. Return this mixture to batter and fold gently using no more than 8 to 10 strokes. Pour into prepared pan, spreading gently. Bake until tester inserted in center of cake comes out clean, about 20 minutes.

Sprinkle kitchen towel lightly with powdered sugar. Turn cake out onto towel and let cool.

For coffee cream: Place egg whites in medium bowl of electric mixer. Combine sugar and water in heavy 1-quart saucepan and stir constantly over very low heat until sugar is dissolved. Increase heat and boil rapidly, without stirring, until syrup reaches 242°F on candy thermometer.

Meanwhile, beat egg whites until stiff. Gradually beat in hot syrup. Add coffee powder and continue beating at medium speed until meringue is cool and stands in stiff peaks.

Beat ½ cup cream until soft peaks form. Add vanilla and beat until stiff.

Cut cooled cake into 3 rectangles measuring approximately 3¼ × 14½ inches. Place 1 piece on cardboard or serving plate. Fold whipped cream into coffee meringue, blending thoroughly. Spread about ½ cup coffee cream evenly over cake. Top with second layer and spread with another ½ cup cream. Place third layer on top and use remaining cream to frost top and sides.

Whip remaining ½ cup cream until stiff. Spoon into pastry bag fitted with decorative tip and pipe down center of cake. If desired, decorate with candy coffee beans just before serving.

Praline Jewel Box with Fresh Berries

8 servings

Sponge Cake
6 eggs, separated, room temperature
¾ cup sugar
1 tablespoon fresh lemon juice
1 teaspoon vanilla
Pinch of salt
Pinch of cream of tartar
1 cup all purpose flour

Praline
2 cups sugar
½ cup sliced almonds, toasted

2 tablespoons amaretto
2 tablespoons raspberry liqueur
¼ cup red currant jelly

Pastry Cream
5 egg yolks, room temperature
½ cup sugar
¼ cup all purpose flour
2 cups milk, heated
1 teaspoon vanilla

4 cups whole strawberries, hulled
2 cups blackberries
2 cups raspberries
Fresh mint sprigs
Whipped cream

For cake: Preheat oven to 350°F. Butter and flour 10-inch springform pan. Using electric mixer, beat yolks with ¼ cup sugar until slowly dissolving ribbon forms when beaters are lifted. Blend in lemon juice and vanilla. Using clean, dry beaters, beat whites with salt and cream of tartar until soft peaks form. Add remaining ½ cup sugar 1 tablespoon at a time and beat until stiff and shiny. Gently fold whites and flour alternately into yolk mixture. Turn into prepared pan, smoothing top. Tap pan against counter to eliminate air pockets. Bake until cake is golden brown and top springs back when lightly touched, 35 to 40 minutes. Cool completely in pan on rack. Remove springform. (*Cake can be prepared 2 days ahead and refrigerated.*)

Using long serrated knife, cut 1-inch-thick "lid" off top of cake. Hollow out bottom, leaving ½-inch-thick shell.

For praline: Heat sugar in heavy skillet over low heat until dissolved, swirling pan occasionally. Increase heat and cook until candy thermometer registers 310°F (hard-crack stage). Remove from heat. Stir in almonds; mixture will bubble. Carefully ladle hot praline over top and sides of lid and sides and top edges of shell. Cool completely.

Sprinkle inside of lid and shell with liqueurs. Spread with jelly. (*Cake can be prepared 1 day ahead to this point. Store at room temperature.*)

For cream: Whisk yolks and sugar in heavy medium saucepan until thick and light. Stir in flour. Gradually whisk in milk. Place over medium-high heat and bring to boil. Reduce heat and simmer until mixture is very thick, whisking constantly, about 5 minutes. Blend in vanilla. Remove from heat. Press plastic wrap onto surface of cream to prevent skin from forming. (*Can be prepared 1 day ahead. Cool completely, cover and refrigerate.*)

Set shell on serving platter. Fill with pastry cream to ¼ inch of top. Refrigerate until ready to serve. (*Can be filled up to 6 hours ahead.*) Keep praline-covered lid at room temperature.

Just before serving, arrange berries decoratively in cream. Tilt lid against shell to show fruit. Garnish with mint. Pass whipped cream separately.

Spanish Cream Torte

8 servings

Torte
- 5 ounces (1 cup) unblanched almonds, toasted
- 2 slices white bread
- 2 tablespoons all purpose flour
- 1 teaspoon cinnamon
- 7 eggs, separated, room temperature
- 1 cup sugar
- 1 teaspoon vanilla
- ½ teaspoon almond extract
- ¼ teaspoon cream of tartar

  Powdered sugar

Spanish Cream
- ½ cup (1 stick) unsalted butter
- ⅔ cup sugar
- 1 egg
- 1 egg yolk
- 2 tablespoons brandy
- 1 teaspoon vanilla
- ¼ teaspoon orange extract
- 1 cup plus 2 tablespoons whipping cream

Garnish
- ⅔ cup orange marmalade
- 1 tablespoon brandy
- ⅓ cup cream Sherry

- 1 navel orange, peeled and sliced
- ¼ cup unblanched almonds, toasted and chopped

For torte: Position rack in center of oven and preheat to 350°F. Line 17½ × 11½ × 1-inch rimmed baking sheet with foil. Grease and flour foil and rims of sheet, shaking off excess. Grind almonds with bread in processor. Turn into bowl. Stir in flour and cinnamon. Beat yolks and ¼ cup sugar in large bowl of electric mixer until light and fluffy. Blend in vanilla and almond extract. Using clean dry beaters, beat whites with cream of tartar until soft peaks form. Add remaining sugar 1 tablespoon at a time and beat until stiff but not dry. Fold ¼ of whites into yolk mixture to lighten. Fold remaining whites into yolk mixture alternately with almond mixture; do not overfold. Pour batter onto prepared sheet, spreading evenly. Bake until edges are dry, about 15 minutes.

Line work surface with waxed paper. Cover paper with powdered sugar. Invert torte onto prepared paper. Peel off foil. Let torte cool. Trim off ⅓ inch from all sides. Cut torte in half crosswise. Cut each piece in half crosswise.

For cream: Combine butter, sugar, egg and yolk in heavy medium saucepan over medium-high heat and whisk until butter melts, sugar dissolves and mixture is light and fluffy, about 5 minutes. Transfer to bowl. Set in larger bowl filled with water and ice and let cool until thick and stiff, stirring occasionally. Blend in brandy, vanilla and orange extract. Beat cream to stiff peaks. Gently beat in egg mixture. Cover and refrigerate at least 1 hour.

For garnish: Heat marmalade and brandy in heavy small saucepan over low heat until marmalade melts, stirring occasionally. Set 1 torte layer on platter. Sprinkle with Sherry. Brush with marmalade. Spread with ⅓-inch-thick layer of cream. Repeat layering with remaining ingredients, ending with cream. Chill torte at least 4 hours.

Before serving, arrange orange slices atop cake; sprinkle with almonds.

Orangen Torte

8 to 10 servings

Orange Curd
3/4 cup fresh orange juice
1/4 cup fresh lemon juice
2 teaspoons cornstarch
1/2 cup (1 stick) unsalted butter, melted
6 tablespoons sugar
3 eggs, room temperature
1 egg yolk, room temperature

Orange Sponge Cake
4 egg yolks, room temperature
11 tablespoons sugar
2 tablespoons orange liqueur
1 tablespoon hot water
1 teaspoon vanilla
3/4 teaspoon grated orange peel

3/4 teaspoon ground cardamom
8 drops almond extract
5 egg whites, room temperature
Pinch of salt
Pinch of cream of tartar

1/2 cup sifted all purpose flour
1/2 cup sifted cake flour
2 tablespoons (1/4 stick) butter, melted and cooled

6 tablespoons orange liqueur

1 1/2 cups whipping cream
2 tablespoons sugar
1 1/2 cups peeled orange sections
Flower leaves (garnish)

For curd: Mix juices with cornstarch in heavy saucepan until dissolved. Whisk in butter, sugar, eggs and yolk until smooth. Place over low heat and stir until mixture is thickened to consistency of thin yogurt, 15 to 20 minutes; *do not boil* (curd may be lumpy). Cool, then refrigerate until thoroughly chilled, preferably overnight; if butter begins to separate out, whisk curd occasionally to reblend.

For cake: Position rack in center of oven and preheat to 350°F. Line bottoms of two 9-inch round cake pans with parchment paper. Combine yolks, 3 tablespoons sugar, orange liqueur, hot water, vanilla, orange peel, cardamom and almond extract in large bowl of electric mixer and beat until pale yellow and slowly dissolving ribbon forms when beaters are lifted, about 7 minutes. Beat whites with salt and cream of tartar in another large bowl set over warm water until soft peaks form. Add remaining 8 tablespoons sugar one at a time and beat until meringue is stiff and glossy.

Resift flours together. Gently fold 1/4 of meringue into yolks. Scrape yolk mixture over remaining meringue with spatula, then sift 1/4 of flour over top and fold in. Repeat until all flour is folded in, being careful not to deflate mixture or allow any lumps to remain. Drizzle butter over and gently fold in using 3 to 4 strokes. Pour batter into prepared pans. Bake until top springs back when touched, 20 to 25 minutes, rotating cakes once. Cool on rack.

To assemble: Loosen cakes from pans and turn out onto work surface. Peel off paper. Invert cakes right side up. Using long serrated knife, halve cakes horizontally through center to make 4 layers. Arrange 1 bottom layer cut side up on platter. Sprinkle with 1 tablespoon liqueur. Spread with 1/3 of curd. Top curd with top of remaining cake. Repeat with liqueur and curd. Top with remaining layer flat side up. Press gently to align layers. Wrap cake in plastic and refrigerate at least 6 hours, preferably overnight.

To serve, whip cream with remaining 2 tablespoons sugar and 2 tablespoons orange liqueur to stiff peaks. Reserve 2/3 cup cream. Spread remaining cream smoothly over cake. Spoon reserved whipped cream into pastry bag fitted with star tip. Pipe cream decoratively around sides of cake. Arrange orange sections over top in concentric circles, overlapping slightly. Garnish cake with flower leaves. Serve at room temperature.

Orangeschnitten

*An impressive and
delicious finale.*

12 to 15 servings

Cake
1¼ cups (2½ sticks) plus 1
    tablespoon well-chilled unsalted
    butter, cut into tablespoons

2 cups sifted cake flour
¼ cup sifted cornstarch
1 teaspoon baking powder
1½ cups sugar
    Peel from 1 large orange
    (orange part only)
5 eggs, separated, room
    temperature
1 teaspoon vanilla

Whipped Cream Filling
1 teaspoon unflavored gelatin
4½ teaspoons cold water

4½ teaspoons Grand Marnier
1 teaspoon vanilla
1½ cups well-chilled whipping cream
¼ cup powdered sugar

Chocolate Buttercream
9 ounces bittersweet or semisweet
    chocolate, coarsely chopped
¾ cup (1½ sticks) well-chilled
    unsalted butter, cut into 1-inch
    pieces
6 well-chilled egg yolks
1 tablespoon coffee liqueur
1 teaspoon vanilla
3 tablespoons powdered sugar

Candied Orange Peel*

For cake: Soften butter at room temperature 30 minutes.

Preheat oven to 350°F. Line 10 × 15-inch jelly roll pan with parchment. Sift flour, cornstarch and baking powder together 3 times. Blend ½ cup sugar with orange peel in processor until peel is minced finely and sugar turns orange, stopping twice to scrape down sides of work bowl, about 2 minutes. Add ½ cup sugar and butter. Mix 40 seconds, stopping once to scrape down sides of work bowl. Blend in yolks and vanilla, stopping once to scrape down sides of work bowl.

Using electric mixer, beat whites until soft peaks form. Add remaining ½ cup sugar 1 tablespoon at a time and beat until whites are stiff but not dry. Add ¼ of whites to batter in processor. Blend until just mixed, 5 to 10 seconds. Pour batter over remaining whites. Fold in half of dry ingredients until almost blended. Fold in remaining dry ingredients until just blended. Pour batter into prepared pan, smoothing top. Bake until tester inserted in center comes out clean, 20 to 25 minutes. Cool in pan 5 minutes. Loosen sides with spatula. Invert onto rack, removing paper. Invert onto another rack and cool completely.

For filling: Soften gelatin in water in small bowl. Set bowl in pan of simmering water and stir until gelatin is dissolved. Mix in Grand Marnier and vanilla. Using electric mixer, whip cream until soft peaks form. Beat in sugar and gelatin mixture; continue beating until stiff peaks form.

Cut cake into three 5 × 10-inch rectangles. Remove any crumbs with pastry brush. Set 1 layer on platter. Spread with half of filling. Top with another layer and remaining filling. Arrange remaining cake layer on top.

For buttercream: Heat chocolate in top of double boiler set over barely simmering water until half melted. Remove from over water and stir to melt completely. Transfer to processor. Arrange butter in circle atop chocolate. Blend just until smooth. Add yolks and blend until smooth, stopping once to scrape down sides of work bowl. With machine running, pour liqueur and vanilla through feed tube. Stop and scrape down sides of bowl. Mix in sugar until just combined.

Set aside 1½ cups buttercream. Spread remaining buttercream on sides and top of cake. Arrange candied orange peel in strip down center of cake. Spoon reserved buttercream into pastry bag fitted with small star tip. Pipe buttercream along top and bottom edges of cake. Refrigerate cake 3 hours to firm. (*Can be prepared 1 day ahead.*) Let stand at room temperature 45 minutes before serving.

*Candied Orange Peel

Makes about ⅓ cup

Peel from 1 large orange
  (orange part only)
½ cup sugar

¼ cup water
Additional sugar

Cut orange peel into very fine julienne. Heat ½ cup sugar and ¼ cup water in heavy small saucepan over low heat, swirling pan occasionally. Add orange peel, increase heat and simmer until peel is tender and translucent, washing down sides of pan with pastry brush dipped in cold water, about 7 minutes. Transfer peel to sheets of waxed paper, using fork (let excess syrup drip back into pan). Separate peel into individual pieces, using toothpicks. Cool completely. Roll peel in additional sugar. Dry completely on plate. (*Can be prepared 2 weeks ahead and stored in airtight container.*)

Lemon Mirror Cake

16 servings

Almond Biscuit
1⅓ cups almond meal
  1 cup plus 2 tablespoons sugar
  4 extra-large eggs, room
    temperature
  4 egg whites, room temperature
    Pinch of cream of tartar
  7 tablespoons sifted cake flour
  3 tablespoons unsalted butter,
    melted and cooled

Lemon Syrup
  ⅓ cup water
  ¼ cup sugar
  1 tablespoon finely grated
    lemon peel
  3 tablespoons strained fresh
    lemon juice

Lemon Bavarian
1½ tablespoons unflavored gelatin
  ½ cup strained fresh lemon juice
1¾ cups milk

  1 tablespoon finely grated
    lemon peel
  5 egg yolks, room temperature
  ⅔ cup sugar
  ⅛ teaspoon salt

1¼ cups whipping cream
  ⅛ to ¼ teaspoon lemon extract
    (optional)

Lemon Mirror
1½ teaspoons unflavored gelatin
  2 tablespoons cold water
  ¾ cup boiling water
  ⅓ cup sugar
    Pinch of salt
  ¼ cup strained fresh lemon juice
    Few drops of yellow food
    coloring (optional)

  Lemon leaves and blossoms
  (optional garnish)

For biscuit: Preheat oven to 450°F. Butter and flour 11 × 17-inch jelly roll pan. Line bottom of pan with parchment paper; butter and flour paper. Combine almond meal and 9 tablespoons sugar in large bowl. Beat in eggs one at a time and continue beating until mixture is light and thick, about 5 minutes. Beat whites with cream of tartar in another large bowl until soft peaks form. Gradually add remaining 9 tablespoons sugar, beating until whites are stiff and glossy; do not overbeat. Fold ¼ of whites into almond mixture. Resift flour over mixture, then fold in carefully. Fold in remaining whites. Blend ½ cup of batter into butter. Fold back into batter. Spread evenly on prepared pan. Bake until cake is very light brown, about 10 minutes; do not overbake or cake will crack when handling. Cool completely. Invert onto work surface and peel off parchment. Cut out two 8-inch circles. Wrap in plastic.

For syrup: Cook water, sugar and lemon peel in heavy small saucepan over low heat until sugar dissolves, swirling pan occasionally. Increase heat, bring to boil and let boil 1 minute. Remove from heat and stir in lemon juice. Cool to room temperature.

For bavarian: Oil sides of 9½ × 2½-inch springform pan. Cut out cardboard circle to fit bottom. Wrap in foil and press into pan. Line sides of pan with plastic wrap, smoothing carefully. Soften gelatin in lemon juice. Bring milk and lemon peel to boil in heavy large saucepan. Beat yolks, sugar and salt in mixer bowl until lemon colored. Whisk in milk. Return mixture to saucepan and stir over medium-low heat until custard is thick enough to coat back of spoon, about 8 minutes; do not boil. Strain through fine sieve into bowl. Set in larger bowl filled with ice. Stir in softened gelatin. Cool mixture until texture resembles slightly whipped cream, stirring occasionally, about 20 minutes.

Beat cream to soft peaks. Fold into cooled custard. Add lemon extract if stronger lemon flavor is desired.

To assemble: Place 1 cake circle in prepared pan. Brush lightly with some of syrup. Pour half of bavarian cream over (cream will surround edges of cake). Gently place second cake circle in center of cream. Brush cake lightly with some of syrup (there will be leftover syrup; do not soak cake). Pour remaining bavarian over, filling pan to ¼ inch of top; smooth surface. Refrigerate for 3 hours.

For mirror: Soften gelatin in cold water in small bowl. Add boiling water and stir until gelatin is dissolved. Add sugar and salt and stir until dissolved. Blend in lemon juice and food coloring. Set bowl in larger bowl filled with ice and let stand until mixture is syrupy and begins to thicken, stirring occasionally, about 30 minutes; do not let set. Brush paper-thin layer of mixture over top of cake. Refrigerate until set. Pour second layer over; total thickness should not be more than 3/16 inch. Refrigerate until mirror is set.

To serve: Carefully release springform; slide cake out. Smooth side of cake with warm, narrow, stainless steel spatula. Garnish cake with lemon leaves and blossoms if desired.

Anise Almond Torte

8 to 10 servings

Torte
1 cup (2 sticks) unsalted butter, room temperature
1 cup almond paste, room temperature
¾ cup sugar
5 eggs, room temperature
2 tablespoons anise liqueur
1½ teaspoons crushed aniseed
1 teaspoon vanilla
1½ cups all purpose flour
1 teaspoon baking powder
½ teaspoon salt

Lemon Meringue Buttercream
½ cup water
Pinch of salt
1 cup sugar
½ cup (generous) egg whites, room temperature (about 4)

1½ cups (3 sticks) unsalted butter, room temperature, creamed until light
4 to 5 tablespoons fresh lemon juice (or to taste)
3 tablespoons anise liqueur
1 tablespoon honey
1 teaspoon grated lemon peel

1 cup toasted blanched almonds, chopped
Candied violets
(optional garnish)

Lemon Mirror Cake

Counterclockwise from top:
Viva Cake of Joy; Mincemeat Torte with
Bourbon Sauce; Individual Baked
Alaska; Pears Poached in Cabernet and
Coriander with Riesling Sauce and Cor-
nets with Chestnut Mousse; Frozen
Chartreuse-Mint Chocolate Soufflé

Rudi Legname

Poached Apples with Cider Sorbet and Caramel Dome

*Opposite page, clockwise from top left:
Chocolate Cheese Torte; Orangen Torte;
Tyrolean Nuss Torte; Anise Almond
Torte; Dios Patko; Rigó Jancsi; Sabayon
Cream and Strawberry Tart; Cointreau
Soufflé in Puff Pastry*

Danish Othello Cake

Chef Besson's Chilled Apple Charlotte with Raspberry Sauce

Jerry Friedman

For torte: Preheat oven to 300°F. Butter and lightly flour angel food cake pan or savarin mold about 5 inches deep, 9¾ inches in diameter. Cream butter with almond paste in large bowl of electric mixer about 3 minutes. Gradually add sugar, beating until very light in color. Beat in eggs one at a time, then mix in liqueur, aniseed and vanilla. Sift flour with baking powder and salt. Add dry ingredients to egg mixture and stir until smooth. Spoon batter into prepared pan. Bake until cake is golden, pulls away slightly from edges of pan and tester inserted in center comes out clean, 50 to 60 minutes. Cool 1 hour. Loosen cake from pan and turn out onto rack. Cover; let stand at room temperature 1 day.

For buttercream: Combine water and salt in heavy small saucepan over low heat. Add sugar and swirl pan gently until syrup is dissolved. Increase heat to medium and cook without stirring until syrup registers 240°F on candy thermometer (soft-ball stage). Meanwhile, beat egg whites in large bowl until soft peaks form.

Remove syrup from heat and let stand until thermometer registers 242°F to 244°F. Very slowly beat syrup into egg whites at medium speed; mixture should be hot and glossy. Let cool to room temperature, beating frequently.

Beat creamed butter into egg white mixture 1 tablespoon at a time at medium speed. Continue beating until consistency of mayonnaise, about 5 minutes. (*If buttercream looks curdled, place briefly over warm water. Remove from heat and beat until smooth. If too soft or melted, refrigerate buttercream until chilled, then beat until smooth.*) Mix in 4 tablespoons lemon juice with liqueur and honey. Taste and add more lemon juice if desired. Set aside 1 cup buttercream for garnish. Blend lemon peel into remaining buttercream. Cover all buttercream and refrigerate. Before using, let stand at room temperature until spreadable.

To assemble, halve cake horizontally using long serrated knife. Transfer bottom to round 10-inch cake cardboard or tart pan liner. Whisk buttercream until smooth. Spread ½-inch-thick layer of buttercream over bottom. Set remaining layer on top. Spread very thin layer of buttercream (crumb coat) over entire surface of cake. Freeze 10 to 15 minutes.

Spread remaining buttercream smoothly over cake using warm spatula (a cake turntable facilitates frosting). Spoon reserved 1 cup buttercream into pastry bag fitted with No. 4 tip. Pipe buttercream in 2 concentric circles around top. Pat almonds around sides. Garnish top with candied violets if desired. Refrigerate. Let stand at room temperature about 30 minutes before serving.

Gâteau Poire Williams

This cake is a spectacular combination of poached pears, chocolate, whipped cream and pear eau-de-vie.

8 to 10 servings

4 eggs
2 egg yolks
⅔ cup sugar
¾ cup plus 1 tablespoon all purpose flour
7 tablespoons cornstarch
2 tablespoons unsweetened cocoa powder

3½ tablespoons poire Williams (pear eau-de-vie)

4 poached pears, halved and patted dry
7 tablespoons water
1 tablespoon unflavored gelatin
5½ ounces semisweet chocolate, melted
2 cups whipping cream, whipped

Chocolate sprinkles
Unsweetened cocoa powder
Whipped cream (garnish)

Preheat oven to 375°F. Line bottom of 9-inch round cake pan with parchment paper. Combine eggs, yolks and sugar in large bowl of electric mixer. Set over hot, but not boiling, water and whisk gently (just enough to keep mixture moving) until warm to touch. Remove from over hot water and immediately begin beating at next to highest speed until completely cooled and tripled in volume, about 5 to 6 minutes. Sift flour, cornstarch and cocoa powder together. Resift over cooled egg mixture in 4 batches, folding in gently after each addition; *do not overmix.* Pour mixture into prepared pan. Bake until tester inserted in center comes out clean, about 25 to 30 minutes. Let cake cool in pan 15 minutes. Carefully invert cake onto wire rack and let cool completely.

Lightly grease 9-inch springform pan. Set cake in pan. Brush poire Williams over top. Arrange pears rounded side up in spoke pattern atop cake, with narrow ends at center. Combine water and gelatin in small saucepan over low heat and stir until dissolved. Remove from heat. Add melted chocolate and blend well. Transfer to large bowl and cool. Fold in whipped cream. Spread over pears. Chill until completely set.

Remove sides of pan. Pat chocolate sprinkles in strip, about 1 inch high, around bottom of cake. Cut circle of cardboard about 3 inches in diameter and place over cake in center. Sprinkle cocoa powder around circle to cover outer rim of cake completely. Carefully remove cardboard. Pipe about 10 rosettes of whipped cream around outside edge of top of cake on top of cocoa powder. Chill until ready to serve.

Danish Othello Cake

12 to 16 servings

Sponge Cake
- 4 extra-large eggs, room temperature
- 1 cup sugar
- 1¼ cups sifted all purpose flour
- 2 teaspoons baking powder
- ¼ cup lukewarm milk (95°F)
- ¼ cup (½ stick) butter, melted
- 1 tablespoon grated orange peel

Macaroon Layer
- ¾ cup (3½ ounces) blanched almonds, toasted and finely ground
- ⅓ cup sugar
- 1 teaspoon baking powder
- 2 egg whites, room temperature
- Pinch of cream of tartar

Vanilla Custard
- 1½ cups half and half or milk
- 4 egg yolks, room temperature
- 2 tablespoons sugar
- 1½ tablespoons cornstarch
- 1 teaspoon vanilla
- ½ cup whipping cream, whipped to soft peaks

Chocolate Icing
- 6 ounces semisweet chocolate, coarsely chopped
- 60 whole blanched almonds
- 3 tablespoons (¼ stick) unsalted butter, room temperature
- 1¼ cups powdered sugar, sifted
- 3 tablespoons double-strength coffee
- 1½ tablespoons dark rum
- Almond Paste Border*
- ½ cup well-chilled whipping cream
- 1 tablespoon powdered sugar

For cake: Preheat oven to 350°F. Line bottom of two 9-inch round cake pans with parchment; grease parchment. Gently whisk eggs with sugar in large bowl of electric mixer set over hot water over low heat until just warm, about 3 minutes. Remove from over water. Beat at high speed of electric mixer until almost tripled in volume and consistency of whipped cream, about 6 minutes. Resift flour with baking powder. Gently fold into egg mixture alternately with lukewarm milk in 3 batches. Fold in butter and orange peel. Divide batter between prepared pans. Bake until cake is golden and springs back when touched in center, 18 to 20 minutes. Cool in pans on rack. (*Can be prepared 1 day ahead.*)

For macaroon layer: Preheat oven to 350°F. Grease 9-inch round cake pan. Line bottom with parchment. Combine almonds, sugar and baking powder in small bowl. Beat whites with cream of tartar in another bowl until stiff but not dry. Fold in almond mixture. Spread in prepared pan. Bake until top is dry, 20 to 25 minutes. Cool completely in pan on rack. (*Can be prepared 1 day ahead. Wrap tightly.*)

For custard: Combine half and half, yolks, sugar and cornstarch in heavy small saucepan over medium heat. Cook until mixture just comes to boil and thickens, whisking constantly. Cover and cool to room temperature. Stir in vanilla. (*Can be prepared 1 day ahead and refrigerated. Bring to room temperature before using.*) Whisk custard to loosen, then fold in whipped cream.

To assemble: Invert 1 sponge layer onto serving platter; remove paper. Spread half of custard over layer. Invert macaroon layer onto custard, removing paper. Spread with remaining custard. Invert second sponge layer on top, removing paper. (*Can be prepared 1 day ahead. Cover and refrigerate.*)

For icing: Melt chocolate in small bowl set over pan of hot water over low heat. Line large plate with waxed paper. Dip tips of 30 almonds in chocolate and place on paper. Set aside remaining chocolate. Chill almonds until coating is hard.

Meanwhile, mix butter, 1 1/4 cups powdered sugar, coffee and rum into remaining chocolate until mixture is glossy and smooth. Cool until spreadable, about 10 minutes.

Smooth icing over top and sides of cake. Roll up almond paste border, starting at 1 short side. Gently unroll onto side of cake, pressing firmly into icing. Whip cream to soft peaks. Beat in 1 tablespoon powdered sugar. Spoon in 1-inch border around top edge of cake. Press chocolate almonds and plain almonds alternately into cream to resemble wreath. Refrigerate up to 4 hours. Bring to room temperature 20 minutes before serving.

*Almond Paste Border

10 ounces (about 1 1/4 cups) almond paste

1 1/4 cups (about) powdered sugar

1 1/4 teaspoons almond extract
Powdered sugar

Combine almond paste, 1 1/4 cups sugar and extract in small bowl. Press together with hands until mixture forms ball, adding more sugar if sticky. Knead in bowl until pliable, about 2 minutes. Form into 14-inch-long rope. Roll out on surface dusted with powdered sugar to strip 28 inches long and as wide as cake is tall. Trim edges. Score almond paste with crosswise lines spaced 1/4 inch apart.

Blitz Torte

12 servings

Meringue
- 4 egg whites, room temperature
- 1 cup sugar
- ½ teaspoon baking powder

Cake
- ½ cup (1 stick) butter, room temperature
- ½ cup sugar
- 4 egg yolks
- 1 teaspoon vanilla
- 1 cup cake flour
- 2 teaspoons baking powder
- 5 tablespoons milk
- 1 cup chopped pecans

Custard
- 1 cup milk
- 3 tablespoons sugar
- 2 tablespoons all purpose flour
- 2 egg yolks, beaten to blend
- 1 tablespoon butter
- ½ teaspoon vanilla

For meringue: Beat whites in medium bowl of electric mixer until frothy. Blend sugar and baking powder in small bowl. Gradually add to whites and beat until stiff but not dry.

For cake: Preheat oven to 325°F. Grease two 9 × 11-inch metal baking pans. Cream butter with sugar in large bowl. Stir in yolks and vanilla. Sift cake flour and baking powder. Add to butter mixture alternately with milk, beginning and ending with flour. Spoon into prepared pans. Spread meringue over each and top with chopped pecans. Bake until tester inserted in centers comes out clean, about 30 minutes. Cool cakes in pans on wire racks.

For custard: Combine milk, sugar and flour in top of double boiler set over hot but not boiling water. Stir over low heat until mixture thickens and coats back of wooden spoon. Stir in yolks and cook 3 minutes. Mix in butter and vanilla. Remove from over hot water and cool.

Invert 1 cake onto platter, meringue side down. Spread with cooled custard. Arrange other layer atop custard, meringue side up. Serve immediately.

Chocolate Torte with Raspberry Coulis

For an elegant finale, serve the torte with Vanilla Poached Pears (see following recipe).

8 servings

Chocolate Torte
- 9 ounces semisweet chocolate, coarsely chopped
- 3 tablespoons framboise (raspberry eau-de-vie)
- 2 tablespoons milk
- 14 tablespoons (1¾ sticks) unsalted butter, cut into tablespoon pieces, room temperature
- 1 cup sugar
- 13 tablespoons sifted cake flour
- 5 eggs, separated, room temperature

Pinch of salt
Pinch of cream of tartar

Chocolate Glaze
- 6 tablespoons whipping cream
- 2 tablespoons framboise
- 8 ounces semisweet chocolate, coarsely chopped

Raspberry Coulis*
Whipped cream

For torte: Preheat oven to 350°F. Butter 8½ × 4-inch heart-shaped cake pan. Line bottom with parchment paper; butter paper. Dust pan and paper with flour. Melt chocolate with framboise and milk in top of double boiler set over barely simmering water. Stir until smooth. Add butter 1 piece at a time, whisking until melted. Mix in ¾ cup sugar, flour and yolks. Cool slightly.

Beat whites, salt and cream of tartar until soft peaks form. Add remaining ¼ cup sugar 1 tablespoon at a time and beat until stiff but not dry. Whisk chocolate mixture to loosen. Gently fold in ¼ of whites. Fold mixture back into remaining whites. Pour into prepared pan. Bake cake until center feels just firm to touch and only a few crumbs stick to tester inserted into center, about 1¼ hours (top will crack). Cool in pan 15 minutes. Turn out onto rack; remove paper. Turn over again onto another rack. Cool.

For glaze: Scald cream with framboise in heavy small saucepan. Remove from heat. Add chocolate a little at a time, stirring until melted. Cool until thick enough to spread.

Invert cake flat side up onto platter. Slide strips of waxed paper under edges of cake. Spread glaze evenly over top and sides of cake. Discard paper. Refrigerate until glaze is firm, about 30 minutes. Serve at room temperature with coulis and whipped cream.

*Raspberry Coulis

Makes about 2 cups

2 10-ounce packages frozen raspberries, thawed
2 tablespoons sugar

2 teaspoons cornstarch dissolved in 2 tablespoons cold water
2 tablespoons framboise

Simmer raspberries with sugar in heavy small saucepan until softened, stirring occasionally, about 2 minutes. Add cornstarch mixture and stir until translucent, about 30 seconds. Strain sauce through fine sieve, pressing to extract as much pulp as possible. Cool. Mix in framboise. (*Coulis can be prepared 1 day ahead and refrigerated.*)

Vanilla Poached Pears

To prevent discoloration, place peeled pears in a large bowl of water blended with fresh lemon juice.

8 servings

2 cups water
1 cup sugar
1 4-inch vanilla bean, split
4 firm, ripe pears, peeled, halved and cored

2 tablespoons poire Williams (pear eau-de-vie)

Raspberry Coulis (see previous recipe)
Candied violets

Heat water, sugar and vanilla bean in heavy large saucepan over low heat, swirling pan occasionally, until sugar dissolves. Increase heat and boil 5 minutes. Add pears. Cover pan, adjust heat so liquid barely shimmers and cook until pears are just tender, turning occasionally, 4 to 10 minutes depending on ripeness and variety of pears. Transfer poached pears to medium bowl, using slotted spoon.

Boil syrup until reduced to 1 cup, about 10 minutes. Cool to lukewarm. Stir poire Williams into syrup. Pour over pears. Cool completely. (*Can be prepared 1 day ahead and refrigerated.*)

Drain pears. Slice each half lengthwise several times without cutting through narrow end. Spoon coulis onto plates. Fan pears atop coulis. Garnish with candied violets and serve.

Hazelnut Roulade

8 servings

Hazelnut Sponge Cake
½ cup (scant) hazelnuts, toasted and husked
2 tablespoons sugar
1 cup sifted cake flour

6 eggs, room temperature
¾ cup sugar

Powdered sugar

Whipped Cream Filling
½ teaspoon unflavored gelatin
1 tablespoon cold water
½ teaspoon vanilla
1 cup well-chilled whipping cream
3 tablespoons powdered sugar

Hazelnut Praline Buttercream
½ cup (1 stick) well-chilled unsalted butter, cut into 6 pieces
1¼ cups powdered sugar
¼ teaspoon instant coffee powder
1 teaspoon brandy
2 egg yolks
1 teaspoon whipping cream (or more)
⅓ cup Hazelnut Praline*

Hazelnut Praline
8 hazelnuts, toasted and husked

For cake: Preheat oven to 350°F. Butter bottom of 10 × 15-inch jelly roll pan. Line with parchment; butter paper. Finely chop hazelnuts with 2 tablespoons sugar in processor. Transfer to small bowl. Mix in flour.

Combine eggs and ¾ cup sugar in large bowl of electric mixer. Whisk over pan of simmering water until very warm to touch, about 4 minutes. Beat with mixer until tripled in volume, about 10 minutes. Gently fold in nut mixture. Pour batter into prepared pan, smoothing top. Bake until cake is golden brown and center is springy to touch, 18 to 22 minutes.

Dust 14 × 22-inch kitchen towel generously with powdered sugar. Cut around sides of cake using small spatula. Immediately invert cake onto sugared towel. Remove parchment. Dust cake with powdered sugar. Fold one end of towel over 10-inch side of cake and roll up jelly roll fashion, starting at 10-inch end. Cool.

For filling: Soften gelatin in water in small bowl. Set bowl in pan of simmering water and stir until gelatin is dissolved. Add vanilla. Using electric mixer, whip cream until soft peaks form. Beat in sugar and gelatin mixture; continue beating until stiff peaks form. Cover and refrigerate while preparing buttercream.

For buttercream: Soften butter at room temperature 30 minutes.

Mix powdered sugar in processor to remove any lumps. Arrange butter atop sugar in circle. Process until mixture forms ball, about 20 seconds. Dissolve coffee in brandy in small bowl. Mix yolks and 1 teaspoon cream into brandy. With machine running, pour liquid ingredients through feed tube and process until well mixed, 15 to 20 seconds. Scrape down sides of work bowl. Add ⅓ cup praline and blend 5 seconds. If necessary, thin buttercream to spreadable consistency with more cream, adding ½ teaspoon at a time and blending for 5 seconds.

To assemble: Unroll cake (do not flatten completely). Spread with filling. Reroll cake. Arrange seam side down on baking sheet. Spread top and sides with buttercream, leaving ends unfrosted. Sprinkle cake with praline and top with hazelnuts. Chill until frosting is set, at least 3 hours. (*Can be prepared 1 day ahead.*) Trim ends. Let stand at room temperature 15 minutes before serving.

*Hazelnut Praline

Makes about 2 cups

½ cup sugar
2 tablespoons water

½ cup (scant) hazelnuts, toasted and husked

Oil baking sheet. Heat sugar and water in heavy small saucepan over low heat, swirling pan occasionally, until sugar dissolves. Increase heat and bring to boil, washing down sides of pan with pastry brush dipped in cold water. Boil until syrup turns deep golden brown. Mix in nuts. Immediately pour onto prepared sheet. Cool completely.

Break praline into pieces. Pulverize in processor. (*Can be prepared 3 weeks ahead. Refrigerate in airtight container.*)

Dios Patko

A perfect coffee-table treat or brunch dessert, this is best if prepared one day ahead.

12 servings

Pastry
- 2 teaspoons dry yeast
- ½ cup warm milk (105°F to 115°F)
- 2¼ cups all purpose flour
- ½ cup (1 stick) well-chilled unsalted butter, cut into ½-inch pieces
- 2 egg yolks
- 2 tablespoons sugar
- ½ teaspoon salt

Walnut Filling
- 2 cups finely ground walnuts (about 12 ounces)
- 1 cup sugar
- ½ cup whipping cream
- ¼ cup chopped dates or raisins
- ½ teaspoon grated lemon peel
- 1 teaspoon vanilla

- 1 egg white blended with 1 teaspoon water
- Powdered sugar

For pastry: Soften yeast in warm milk in small bowl. Meanwhile, place flour in large bowl. Add butter and blend with fingertips until mixture resembles coarse meal. Blend yolks, sugar and salt with yeast mixture. Stir yolk mixture into flour to form smooth dough. Turn out onto lightly floured surface and knead until smooth, about 10 minutes. Pat dough into 5 × 7-inch rectangle. Wrap in plastic and refrigerate until thoroughly chilled, at least several hours or overnight.

For filling: Combine walnuts, sugar, cream, dates and lemon peel in large saucepan over medium heat and cook until thick and creamy, about 5 minutes. Let cool. Blend in vanilla.

Butter baking sheet. Remove dough from refrigerator and let soften to rolling consistency. Roll out on lightly floured surface to 14 × 18-inch rectangle. Dot filling over dough; spread evenly, leaving 1-inch border on all sides. Moisten border lightly with water. Starting at long side, roll dough up and pinch ends to seal. Tuck under ends. Transfer to prepared baking sheet seam side down. Curl into horseshoe shape. Cover and let stand 30 minutes; dough will rise only slightly.

Preheat oven to 350°F. Brush pastry with egg mixture. Using skewer, pierce top of pastry at 12 even intervals. Bake until well browned (pastry may crack slightly), 35 to 40 minutes. Cool on rack. Dust with powdered sugar. Serve at room temperature. (*Can be prepared several days ahead, covered with plastic wrap and stored at room temperature.*)

Festive Chocolate Cookie Roll

8 servings

Creamy Chocolate Frosting
- 1 cup semisweet chocolate chips
- 2/3 cup firmly packed brown sugar
- 3 ounces cream cheese, room temperature
- 1/2 teaspoon vanilla
- 1/2 teaspoon cinnamon
- Pinch of salt
- 1 egg yolk
- 1 cup whipping cream, whipped

Cake
- 1/3 cup all purpose flour
- 1/2 teaspoon baking powder
- 14 Oreo cookies, crushed
- 5 eggs, separated, room temperature
- 1/2 cup sugar
- 1 teaspoon vanilla

- 2 tablespoons powdered sugar

Cream Filling
- 1 cup whipping cream, whipped
- 1/2 cup slivered almonds, toasted
- 1/4 teaspoon almond extract

Meringue mushrooms

For frosting: Melt chocolate chips in small saucepan over low heat. Combine brown sugar, cream cheese, vanilla, cinnamon and salt in large bowl. Add yolk and beat until fluffy. Stir in chocolate; fold in whipped cream. Chill 1 to 1½ hours or overnight.

For cake: Preheat oven to 350°F. Grease 10½ × 15½-inch jelly roll pan. Line pan with foil; lightly grease foil. Sift flour and baking powder into medium bowl. Stir in cookie crumbs and set aside. Beat yolks with sugar at medium speed in large bowl of electric mixer until just blended. Stir in vanilla and set aside. Beat whites in another bowl until stiff. Stir 1/3 of crumbs into yolk mixture. Gently fold in 1/3 of whites. Repeat twice. Spread batter evenly into prepared pan. Bake until tester inserted in center comes out clean, approximately 15 minutes.

Sprinkle powdered sugar over towel. Remove cake from oven and cover pan with towel, sugar side down, then top with cutting board, if desired. Invert cake onto towel and board or other flat surface. Remove pan and gently peel off foil. Carefully roll up cake starting from short end, using towel as aid. Cool on rack 30 minutes.

For filling: Combine whipped cream, almonds and almond extract in small bowl. Set aside.

To assemble: Unroll cake and remove towel. Spread filling evenly, almost to edges of cake. Gently reroll cake. Transfer to serving platter. Spread frosting over top and ends. Make loglike marks using fork tines. Garnish with meringue mushrooms and refrigerate until ready to serve.

Chocolate Mousse Torte

This ambrosial dessert has a clever method of preparation: Some unbaked batter is used as a frosting and the cooked, meringue-like topping is crumbled and used on the side of the finished cake.

16 to 20 servings

- 1½ cups (3 sticks) unsalted butter
- 12 ounces semisweet chocolate, cut into small pieces
- 12 extra-large egg yolks
- 1¾ cups sugar
- 7 extra-large egg whites

Unsweetened cocoa powder
Powdered sugar

Preheat oven to 325°F. Cut circle of parchment or waxed paper to fit 10-inch springform pan and place in bottom of pan. Melt butter in medium saucepan over low heat. Remove from heat. Add chocolate and stir until melted, about 3 minutes. Let mixture cool slightly, about 2 to 3 minutes. Combine yolks and sugar in large bowl of electric mixer and beat until mixture forms slowly dissolving ribbon when beaters are lifted, about 5 minutes. Add butter and chocolate and mix well. Beat whites in large bowl of electric mixer just beyond point where soft peaks form; do not beat until stiff. Fold whites into chocolate mixture gently but thoroughly. Reserve 1 cup batter for frosting; do not chill. Immediately pour remaining batter into prepared pan. Bake until tester inserted in center comes out clean, about 1 hour and 35 minutes.

Let cake cool 10 minutes. Carefully remove top "crust" with serrated knife and reserve. Using spatula, gently press down sides of cake to even top surface. Let cool 10 minutes more. Invert cake onto platter; top of cake becomes bottom. Let cool completely.

Frost top and sides of cake with reserved 1 cup batter. Crush reserved top crust between 2 sheets of waxed paper using rolling pin. Pat onto sides of cake. Sprinkle cocoa powder over top. Place lace paper doily atop cocoa powder and sprinkle powdered sugar over. Carefully remove doily to leave decorative design. Refrigerate torte until ready to serve.

Donna Torta

12 servings

3/4 cup sugar
4 eggs, separated, room temperature
1/2 cup plus 2 tablespoons (1 1/4 sticks) unsalted butter, room temperature
5 ounces semisweet chocolate, melted
1/2 cup finely ground almonds (about 5 ounces)

2 tablespoons unbleached all purpose flour
7 ounces semisweet chocolate
1 1/2 teaspoons peanut oil
1/4 cup Quick-dipping Fondant*
1/4 cup (about) toasted sliced almonds

Preheat oven to 375°F. Butter and flour 9-inch round cake pan, shaking out excess. Beat sugar and yolks in large bowl of electric mixer until pale yellow and slowly dissolving ribbon forms when beaters are lifted, about 7 minutes. Blend in butter. Mix in melted chocolate, then ground almonds and flour. Beat whites in another large bowl until stiff. Add half of whites to batter and mix at low speed 1 minute. Gently but thoroughly fold in remaining whites. Pour batter into prepared pan. Bake until cake rises to top of pan and is just firm, about 25 minutes. Cool cake completely in pan on wire rack.

Invert cake onto rack set over waxed paper. Melt remaining 7 ounces chocolate in top of double boiler set over hot water. Blend in peanut oil. Remove frosting from heat and stir until almost cool, about 3 minutes. Pour frosting over top of cake, letting it run over sides. Using long spatula, smooth top of cake, then smooth sides. Cool 1 to 2 minutes, smoothing sides once. Cool 2 to 3 more minutes. Meanwhile, working quickly so fondant and frosting do not set, spoon fondant into pastry bag fitted with narrow tip. Pipe fondant onto cake in concentric circles. Run tip of pointed knife over frosting in straight lines from center to edge of cake, rotating cake after each line and spacing evenly (about 1 1/2 inches apart) to form spiderweb pattern. Pat sliced almonds onto sides of cake. Refrigerate. Let stand at room temperature 30 minutes before serving.

*Quick-dipping Fondant

Makes about 1 cup

3/4 cup sugar
6 tablespoons water

2 1/4 teaspoons light corn syrup
3 1/4 cups sifted powdered sugar

Combine sugar, water and syrup in large saucepan over medium heat and cook until clear and syrupy, about 10 minutes. Remove from heat. Let stand until syrup registers 170°F on candy thermometer, about 3 minutes. While syrup is still hot, gradually add 3 cups plus 2 tablespoons powdered sugar, beating until smooth, shiny and lukewarm. If fondant is too thin, gradually add remaining powdered sugar, beating constantly. If too thick, add about ½ teaspoon hot water. Keep fondant at workable consistency by restirring over simmering (not boiling) water if necessary. (*Can be prepared ahead. Let cool, cover and refrigerate, or freeze until ready to use. Reheat over simmering water.*)

Chocolate-Orange Mousse Cake

8 to 10 servings

Cake
5 tablespoons plus 1 teaspoon unsalted butter, room temperature
1⅓ cups sugar
1 teaspoon vanilla
2 large eggs, beaten, minus 1 tablespoon
1½ cups unsweetened cocoa powder
1 cup plus 3 tablespoons all purpose flour
½ teaspoon baking soda
½ teaspoon baking powder
Pinch of salt
1¼ cups milk

Chocolate-Orange Mousse
12 ounces semisweet chocolate, coarsely chopped
2 ounces unsweetened chocolate, coarsely chopped

¼ cup fresh orange juice
1 tablespoon unflavored gelatin

1½ cups whipping cream
3 egg yolks
Finely grated peel of 1 medium orange

5 egg whites, room temperature
¼ cup sugar

Topping
1 cup whipping cream
¼ cup powdered sugar
1 tablespoon vanilla

2 ounces semisweet chocolate, coarsely chopped
2 tablespoons whipping cream

For cake: Preheat oven to 375°F. Line 10 × 15 × 1-inch jelly roll pan with parchment paper or foil. Cream butter in large bowl. Add sugar and vanilla and beat until light and fluffy. Gradually beat in egg. Sift dry ingredients. Blend into butter mixture alternately with milk, beginning and ending with dry ingredients. Pour batter into prepared pan, spreading evenly. Bake until cake springs back when pressed lightly with finger, about 10 to 12 minutes. Turn out onto rack and cool. Peel off parchment.

For mousse: Melt semisweet and unsweetened chocolates in top of double boiler set over gently simmering water. Transfer to large bowl and set aside. Meanwhile, pour orange juice into cup. Sprinkle gelatin over top. Let stand until liquid is completely absorbed, about 5 minutes.

Combine cream and egg yolks in heavy medium saucepan. Place over low heat and cook, stirring constantly, until custard begins to thicken. Remove from heat. Blend in gelatin mixture. Add custard to melted chocolate and mix well. Stir in orange peel. Let mixture cool for 30 minutes.

Beat egg whites in large bowl of electric mixer at high speed until soft peaks form. Add sugar and continue beating until stiff peaks form. Stir ¼ of egg whites into chocolate mixture, then fold in remaining whites. Cover mousse and refrigerate overnight.

For topping: Combine 1 cup cream with powdered sugar and vanilla in medium bowl and whip to soft peaks.

Melt coarsely chopped chocolate with 2 tablespoons cream in top of double boiler set over gently simmering water. Remove from heat and stir through several times to blend.

To assemble: Cut cake crosswise into 4 equal rectangles. Place 1 rectangle on platter. Gently spread ¼-inch-thick layer of mousse over top, being careful not to deflate mousse. Repeat layering cake and mousse, ending with fourth cake layer. Freeze cake 1 hour. Cover top and sides of cake with remaining mousse, spreading evenly.

Pipe rosettes of whipped cream topping over cake, covering completely. Drizzle chocolate cream mixture over whipped cream. Refrigerate cake until ready to serve.

Rigó Jancsi

A Hungarian specialty traditionally prepared with apricot jam. Whip the egg whites over warm water to dissolve the sugar completely and get the maximum volume.

12 servings

Mocha Cake
4½ ounces semisweet chocolate, finely chopped
¾ ounce unsweetened chocolate, finely chopped
5 eggs, separated, room temperature
9 tablespoons sugar
¾ teaspoon instant espresso powder dissolved in 1½ tablespoons hot water (or 1½ tablespoons very strong coffee)
1 teaspoon vanilla
Large pinch of salt
Pinch of cream of tartar

Chocolate Ganache
1¾ cups whipping cream

2¼ ounces semisweet chocolate, finely chopped
1¼ ounces unsweetened chocolate, finely chopped
¼ cup sugar
¾ teaspoon vanilla
Pinch of salt

⅓ cup raspberry jam
1 tablespoon water
Unsweetened cocoa powder

Chocolate Glaze
4 ounces semisweet chocolate, coarsely chopped
2 tablespoons whipping cream
2 tablespoons water

For cake: Preheat oven to 375°F. Line 10½ × 15-inch jelly roll pan with parchment paper or greased and floured waxed paper. Melt chocolates in small saucepan over hot water. Let cool slightly. Meanwhile, beat yolks with 2 tablespoons sugar in large bowl of electric mixer until pale yellow and slowly dissolving ribbon forms when beaters are lifted. Blend in espresso, vanilla and melted chocolate. Beat whites with salt and cream of tartar to soft peaks in large bowl set over warm water. Add remaining 7 tablespoons sugar 1 tablespoon at a time, beating meringue until stiff and glossy.

Fold ¼ of meringue into chocolate mixture to lighten. Gently fold in remaining meringue until just blended (streaks of white may remain). Turn batter into prepared pan; smooth surface with spatula. Bake 10 minutes. Reduce oven temperature to 350°F and continue baking until top of cake cracks when lightly pressed, 5 to 10 minutes. Cool in pan on rack.

For ganache: Warm cream to about 100°F in medium saucepan. Remove from heat. Add chocolates, sugar, vanilla and salt and let stand until chocolate is almost melted. Stir with whisk until smooth and completely melted. (*Depending on type of chocolate used, some flecks may remain.*) Refrigerate until thoroughly chilled, about 3 to 4 hours, preferably overnight.

To assemble: Loosen edges of cake from pan. Melt jam with 1 tablespoon water until smooth. Dust top of cake generously with cocoa. Cover with waxed paper. Set baking sheet over top, then flip pan over. Peel off parchment paper. Cut cake crosswise in half. Refrigerate until chilled. Meanwhile, beat ganache until just thick and spreadable; do not overbeat.

Spoon ganache over jam-coated cake layer. Using metal spatula, spread ganache evenly over top of cake flush with sides. Chill while preparing glaze.

Meanwhile, for glaze: Heat chocolate, cream and water in small saucepan over hot water until melted and smooth. Remove cake from refrigerator. Slide flat baking sheet under remaining cake layer (leaving waxed paper on baking sheet), then carefully slide cake onto ganache layer (be careful to position cake directly over ganache as layers cannot be moved again). Press top gently with hands to even. Pour chocolate glaze over top and smooth with spatula (top layer does not have to be perfectly smooth as sides will be trimmed and cake cut into pieces). Chill at least 2 hours.

To serve, trim off rough edges using long, thin knife (dip knife in hot water, then wipe dry between cuts to facilitate). To slice, push serrated knife through cake from top to bottom (do not use back and forth motion).

Chestnut Chocolate Cake

12 servings

Chocolate Cake
8 ounces semisweet chocolate, finely chopped
¼ cup cold espresso
4 eggs, separated, room temperature
10 tablespoons (1¼ sticks) unsalted butter, cut into 10 pieces
1 tablespoon Cognac

Pinch of salt
Pinch of cream of tartar
½ cup sugar
½ cup cornstarch

Ganache
¾ cup whipping cream
8 ounces semisweet chocolate, finely chopped
1 tablespoon Cognac

6 glacéed chestnuts, halved

Glaze
1 cup whipping cream
10 ounces semisweet chocolate, finely chopped
1 tablespoon Cognac

1 candied violet

For cake: Preheat oven to 350°F. Grease two 8-inch round cake pans. Line with parchment or foil; butter and lightly flour paper or foil. Melt chocolate with espresso in double boiler over gently simmering water. Stir until smooth. Remove from over water. Stir in yolks one at a time. Place over water and warm just until yolks thicken slightly, about 1 minute. Remove from over water. Stir in butter 1 piece at a time. Blend in Cognac.

Using electric mixer, beat whites in large bowl with salt and cream of tartar until soft peaks form. Gradually add sugar, beating until stiff but not dry. Beat in cornstarch. Stir ¼ of whites into chocolate mixture to loosen. Fold in remaining whites. Pour into prepared pans. Bake until edges are firm but inside is still slightly creamy, about 25 minutes. Cool in pans on rack; cakes will deflate. Remove from pans. Brush off crumbs.

For ganache: Bring cream to boil in heavy small saucepan over low heat. Remove from heat. Pour into mixing bowl. Add chocolate, cover and let stand 5 minutes. Stir gently until chocolate is melted. Add Cognac. Refrigerate until mixture just begins to thicken. Beat with electric mixer on medium-high speed until ganache is light, increased in volume and just beginning to form soft peaks.

Cut out piece of cardboard slightly smaller than cake. Wrap in foil. Set on rack. Top with 1 cake layer. Spread evenly with ganache. Arrange chestnut halves equidistant around outer edge. Top with second cake layer. Press with baking sheet to level. Smooth edges. Refrigerate until ganache is chilled. (*Can be prepared 2 days ahead.*)

For glaze: Bring cream to boil in heavy medium saucepan. Remove from heat. Add chocolate, cover and let stand 5 minutes. Stir gently until chocolate is melted. Mix in Cognac. Cool glaze until just warm to touch. Reserve ½ cup. Pour remainder over cake, tilting back and forth so glaze drops to coat sides. Smooth with spatula. Transfer cake to platter. Cool reserved glaze until set.

Spoon half of reserved glaze into pastry bag fitted with small plain tip. Pipe crisscross pattern over top and sides of cake. Fit bag with leaf tip. Spoon in remaining glaze. Pipe leaves around bottom. Set violet in center.

Derby Dacquoise Cake

12 servings

Pecan Dacquoise
- ¾ cup lightly toasted pecans
- 1 cup sugar
- 4 egg whites, room temperature
- Pinch of salt
- Pinch of cream of tartar

Génoise
- 6 eggs, room temperature
- 1 cup sugar
- 1 tablespoon vanilla

- 1⅓ cups cake flour
- ¼ teaspoon salt
- ½ cup (1 stick) butter, melted and clarified

Chocolate Buttercream
- 2 cups (4 sticks) unsalted butter, room temperature

- 1⅓ cups sugar
- ⅔ cup water
- 8 egg yolks, room temperature
- 1 teaspoon vanilla
- 6 ounces unsweetened chocolate, melted and cooled to lukewarm

Bourbon Syrup
- ¼ cup sugar
- ¼ cup water
- 3 tablespoons bourbon

- ½ cup pecan halves
- ½ cup semisweet chocolate chips

For dacquoise: Preheat oven to 300°F. Grease baking sheets. Line with parchment; grease and flour paper. Trace three 8-inch circles on sheets. Finely grind pecans with half of sugar in processor. Using electric mixer, beat whites in large bowl with salt and cream of tartar until soft peaks form. Gradually add remaining sugar and beat until stiff but not dry. Gently fold in pecans. Spread mixture evenly into circles on sheets. Bake until light brown and crisp, about 1 hour. Cool 2 minutes on sheets. Transfer to racks using broad spatula and cool completely. (*Can be prepared 1 week ahead and stored in airtight container.*)

For génoise: Position rack in center of oven and preheat to 350°F. Butter two 8-inch round cake pans. Line bottoms with parchment or foil; butter and flour parchment paper or foil.

Whisk eggs and sugar in large bowl set over pan of gently simmering water until mixture feels warm to touch. Remove from over water. Add vanilla. Beat with electric mixer until slowly dissolving ribbon forms when beaters are lifted, about 10 minutes.

Sift together flour and salt. Sift flour into egg mixture in 3 additions, folding gently and simultaneously rotating bowl. Add small amount of batter to butter and fold until well blended. Gently fold butter mixture back into batter; do not overfold. Pour into prepared pans, spreading evenly. Tap pans once on counter to eliminate air pockets. Bake until génoise begins to pull away from sides of pan and top feels springy to touch, about 25 minutes. Cool 10 minutes in pans. Invert génoise onto rack. Peel off paper and cool completely. (*Can be prepared 2 days ahead and stored at room temperature, or several weeks ahead and frozen.*)

For buttercream: Cream butter to consistency of mayonnaise. Cook sugar and water in heavy medium saucepan over low heat until sugar dissolves, swirling pan occasionally. Increase heat, bring to boil and cook until candy thermometer registers 234°F (soft-ball stage). Using electric mixer, beat yolks in large bowl until thick and light. Add sugar syrup in thin stream, beating at high speed. Continue beating until mixture cools to room temperature. Blend in vanilla. Reduce speed to low. Beat in half of creamed butter a little at a time. Beat in melted chocolate. Beat in remaining butter a little at a time. (*Can be prepared 1 week ahead and refrigerated or several weeks ahead and frozen. Bring to room temperature before using. Rebeat with wooden spoon until soft and shiny.*)

For syrup: Cook sugar and water in heavy small saucepan over low heat until sugar dissolves, swirling pan occasionally. Increase heat and bring to boil. Cool. Stir in bourbon. Brush each génoise with half of syrup.

To assemble: Trim dacquoise to same size as génoise. Divide buttercream into 6 portions. Cut out piece of cardboard slightly smaller than génoise. Wrap in foil. Affix 1 dacquoise layer to foil with teaspoon of buttercream.

Spread dacquoise with portion of buttercream. Top with 1 génoise layer. Spread with portion of buttercream. Top with second dacquoise layer. Spread with portion of buttercream. Top with second génoise layer. Spread with portion of buttercream. Top with third dacquoise layer. Spread top and sides of cake with portion of buttercream. Place remaining portion of buttercream in pastry bag fitted with star tip. Pipe rosettes around top and bottom edges. Top each rosette alternately with pecan half and chocolate chip. Set cake on platter. Refrigerate until buttercream is firm. Bring to room temperature before serving.

Bûche de Noël (Christmas Yule Log)

This lighter version of the traditional French cake is made without flour. It is decorated with holly leaves and berries made from tinted marzipan.

8 to 10 servings

Cake
 6 egg yolks
 ½ cup powdered sugar, sifted
 1 teaspoon vanilla
 6 tablespoons unsweetened cocoa powder, sifted
 ⅛ teaspoon salt
 6 egg whites
  Pinch of cream of tartar

Buttercream
 1 cup sugar
 ⅓ cup water

 2 eggs
 1 cup (2 sticks) unsalted butter, room temperature
 ½ cup (1 stick) unsalted margarine, room temperature
 4 ounces unsweetened chocolate, melted, *or* 1 cup unsweetened cocoa powder

Marzipan
Green and red paste food coloring
Powdered sugar

For cake: Preheat oven to 325°F. Line jelly roll pan with parchment, extending several inches over ends; oil well. Beat yolks until light. Add sugar gradually and beat until very creamy. Blend in vanilla, then cocoa and salt. Beat whites with cream of tartar until stiff but not dry. Fold into cocoa mixture. Spread in prepared pan. Bake until tester inserted in center comes out clean, about 25 minutes.

Immediately turn out onto damp towel lined with parchment. Peel paper from cake. Roll cake lengthwise and let cool to room temperature.

For buttercream: Combine sugar and water in small saucepan and cook to soft-ball stage (234°F on candy thermometer). Meanwhile, break eggs into medium bowl. Beating constantly, gradually add hot syrup to eggs and beat until cold. Thoroughly cream butter and margarine in large bowl. Beat in egg mixture, then blend in chocolate or cocoa.

Unroll cooled cake. Spread with half of buttercream. Roll again and spread most of remaining buttercream over top and sides. Use fork to make marks resembling bark across top of cake. Slicing diagonally, cut off ends of cake; frost completely with rest of buttercream. Set randomly over cake to resemble knotholes on log; repeat bark pattern on knots.

Tint marzipan with paste food coloring. Roll red-tinted marzipan into small balls to resemble holly berries. Dust work surface with powdered sugar and roll out green marzipan as thinly as possible (if rolling pin sticks, use more powdered sugar). Cut with sharp knife; a sawing motion will make rough edges. Set leaves and berries decoratively on log.

Spiced Chocolate Torte Wrapped in Chocolate Ribbons

12 to 14 servings

Cake
- 1½ cups (3 sticks) butter, room temperature
- 2 cups sugar
- 8 eggs, separated, room temperature
- 10 ounces semisweet chocolate, melted
- 1½ cups finely chopped pecans
- 2 teaspoons vanilla
- 1 teaspoon cinnamon
- 1 teaspoon ground cloves
- 1 teaspoon freshly grated nutmeg
- 1⅓ cups all purpose flour, sifted

  Pinch of salt
  Pinch of cream of tartar

Chocolate Buttercream
- ¾ cup sugar
- ½ cup light corn syrup
- 4 jumbo egg yolks
- 1½ cups (3 sticks) butter, cut into small pieces, room temperature
- 6 ounces semisweet chocolate, melted and cooled
- ¼ cup dark rum

Glaze
- 12 ounces semisweet chocolate
- ¾ cup (1½ sticks) unsalted butter, cut into small pieces
- 2 tablespoons honey
- ¾ teaspoon instant coffee powder

White and Dark Chocolate Ribbons
- 7 ounces white chocolate, broken into pieces
- ¼ cup light corn syrup
- 7 ounces semisweet chocolate, broken into pieces
- ¼ cup light corn syrup

For cake: Position rack in center of oven and preheat to 350°F. Butter and flour three 9-inch round cake pans. Line bottom of each with waxed paper; butter and flour paper.

Cream butter in large bowl of electric mixer. Gradually beat in sugar until smooth. Beat in yolks one at a time. Blend in melted chocolate. Slowly mix in pecans, vanilla and spices. Gently fold in flour in 4 batches (batter will be very thick and dense).

Using electric mixer, beat whites with salt and cream of tartar until medium peaks form. Gently fold ¼ of whites into batter to lighten; then fold in remaining whites. Divide batter among prepared pans, spreading evenly. Bake until toothpick inserted in center of cake comes out clean, 35 to 40 minutes. Run knife around edge of each cake. Let stand 10 minutes. Invert cakes onto racks. Cool to room temperature. (*Can be prepared 2 weeks ahead. Wrap tightly and freeze.*)

For buttercream: Stir sugar and corn syrup in heavy medium saucepan over medium heat until mixture boils. Cook 1 minute. Remove from heat.

Beat yolks with electric mixer until pale and thick. Gradually beat in hot sugar syrup and continue beating until mixture is completely cool, about 5 minutes. Beat in butter 1 piece at a time, incorporating each piece completely before adding next. Blend in melted chocolate, then rum. (*Can be made 2 days ahead and refrigerated.*)

Reserve ½ cup buttercream. Set 1 cake layer flat side up on rack. Spread with half of remaining buttercream. Top with second cake layer. Spread with remaining buttercream. Top with third cake layer. Use reserved ½ cup buttercream to fill in "seam" where layers meet. Freeze cake until buttercream is firm, about 2 hours.

For glaze: Stir all ingredients in top of double boiler over gently simmering water until mixture is smooth and shiny. Remove from over water. Stir until glaze is thickened, about 5 minutes; do not allow to set.

Pour ¾ of glaze over top of cake. Carefully and quickly tilt cake back and forth so glaze coats sides; smooth sides with spatula, adding some of remaining glaze where necessary. Refrigerate cake until glaze is set.

For ribbons: Melt white chocolate in top of double boiler over gently simmering water; stir until smooth. Stir in syrup. Pour onto baking sheet. Refrigerate until firm, 30 to 40 minutes. Transfer to work surface and knead several minutes. Shape into ball. Wrap in plastic. Let at room temperature 1 hour.

Repeat with semisweet chocolate.

Cut white chocolate into 4 pieces. Flatten 1 piece into rectangle. Turn pasta machine to widest setting. Run chocolate through 3 times, folding into thirds before each run. Adjust machine to next narrower setting. Run chocolate through machine without folding. If chocolate is more than ¹⁄₁₆ inch thick, run through next narrower setting. Lay piece on rimless baking sheet. Repeat flattening, folding and rolling with remaining pieces.

Repeat with semisweet chocolate.

Cut four 8 × 1-inch strips from white chocolate and four 8 × ½-inch strips from semisweet chocolate. Center dark chocolate strips on white chocolate strips to form 4 ribbons. Run 1 ribbon from base of cake to center. Arrange remaining 3 ribbons equidistant from each other in same fashion.

Cut ten 6½ × 1-inch strips from white chocolate and ten 6½ × ½-inch strips from semisweet chocolate. Center dark chocolate strips on white chocolate strips to form 10 ribbons. Cut ends off 2 ribbons on diagonal. Starting at center, drape ribbons over top and sides of cake to form "trailers." Fold remaining 8 ribbons in half, layered side out. Cut ends into V shapes. Arrange ribbon halves with V shapes at center of cake to form bow.

Cut one 3 × 1-inch strip of white chocolate and one 3 × ½-inch strip of semisweet chocolate. Center dark chocolate strip on white chocolate strip. Fold in ends and pinch to resemble knot. Place in center of bow. Transfer cake to platter. (*Can be prepared 1 day ahead and refrigerated. Bring cake to room temperature before serving.*)

🍎 *Cheesecakes*

Baklava Cheesecake

Sheets of phyllo pastry are a change-of-pace "crust" for this treat.

16 servings

Cream Cheese Filling
- 2 **pounds (32 ounces) cream cheese, room temperature**
- 1 **cup clover honey**
- ¼ **cup fresh lemon juice**
- 2 **teaspoons vanilla**
- 6 **eggs, room temperature**

- ½ **cup (1 stick) unsalted butter, clarified**
- 1 **pound phyllo pastry sheets**

Baklava Topping
- ½ **cup walnuts**
- ½ **cup blanched almonds**

- 1 **tablespoon sugar**
- 1 **teaspoon cinnamon**
- ½ **cup (1 stick) unsalted butter, clarified**

- ½ **cup sugar**
- ¼ **cup water**
- 1 **tablespoon fresh lemon juice**
- 1 **1½-inch cinnamon stick**
- 1 **tablespoon Cognac**

For filling: Position rack in lower third of oven and preheat to 350°F. Beat cream cheese in large bowl of electric mixer until light and fluffy. Gradually mix in honey, then lemon juice and vanilla. Beat in eggs one at a time until just incorporated. Set aside.

Brush 10-inch springform pan with clarified butter. Arrange 1 phyllo pastry sheet with long edge parallel to edge of surface (cover remaining sheets with dampened towel). Brush left half of sheet with clarified butter and fold right half over. Brush top with butter. Place in prepared pan, buttered side up, leaving 5-inch overhang at one end. Cover with another dampened towel. Butter and fold second phyllo sheet and arrange in pan, overlapping first sheet by 3 inches. Repeat with 4 more sheets, covering entire pan. (Wrap remaining phyllo pastry sheets airtight and refrigerate.)

Stir through filling and pour into crust. Cover filling with overhanging phyllo, squaring at edge of pan. Bake until pastry is light brown and cake is firm to touch, about 50 minutes. Remove pan sides; using toothpick, poke 12 holes in top of cake to allow steam to escape. Cool completely on rack. Refrigerate 2 days to mellow flavors, covering after first day.

For topping: Preheat oven to 350°F. Cover baking sheet with 2 pieces of parchment. Coarsely grind all nuts with 1 tablespoon sugar and 1 teaspoon cinnamon in processor. Stack 10 reserved phyllo pastry sheets on work surface. Set rim of 10-inch springform pan atop pastry. Cut around inside of rim through entire stack using sharp knife, making 10 rounds. Cover rounds with damp towel. Set pan rim on prepared baking sheet. Brush parchment and inside of pan rim with clarified butter. Place 1 pastry round in pan rim and brush with butter. Repeat with 4 more rounds. Spread nut mixture evenly over pastry. Top with remaining 5 pastry rounds, brushing each with butter. Using ruler as guide, cut pastry into 16 wedges with sharp knife. Sprinkle lightly with water. Bake until crisp and golden, about 30 minutes.

Meanwhile, heat ½ cup sugar, water and lemon juice in heavy small saucepan over low heat, swirling pan occasionally, until sugar dissolves. Add cinnamon stick, increase heat to medium and boil until syrupy, about 4 minutes. Remove from heat. When bubbles subside, stir in Cognac.

Flatten pastry atop cake. Remove pan rim from topping. Set topping on cake, using large spatula. Recut wedges. Replace pan rim on assembled cake. Immediately pour on hot syrup. Cool 1 hour. Refrigerate 1 to 6 hours. Let cake stand at room temperature for 20 minutes before serving.

Black Forest Cheesecake

12 to 14 servings

Cherry Topping
1 pound frozen unsweetened cherries, thawed
¼ cup kirsch

¼ cup (about) Morello cherry syrup* or sour cherry syrup

Chocolate Crust
8½ ounces chocolate wafer cookies
6 tablespoons (¾ stick) well-chilled butter, cut into ½-inch pieces

Chocolate Filling
1½ cups whipping cream
12 ounces semisweet chocolate, coarsely chopped

1 pound (16 ounces) cream cheese, room temperature
¾ cup sugar
4 eggs, room temperature
1 teaspoon vanilla

1 cup well-chilled whipping cream
2 tablespoons sugar
1 tablespoon kirsch
Chocolate curls (optional)

For topping: Soak undrained cherries and kirsch in small bowl 6 hours.

Thoroughly drain cherries in strainer set over medium bowl, shaking occasionally, at least 2 hours. Reserve liquid.

Add enough Morello cherry syrup to cherry liquid to measure 1 cup. Pour 6 tablespoons into heavy 8-inch skillet (reserve remaining liquid for filling). Halve cherries and add to skillet. Boil until syrup is thickened and mixture resembles preserves, about 6 minutes. (*Can be prepared 2 days ahead; refrigerate.*)

For crust: Generously butter 9-inch springform pan. Finely crush cookies in processor using on/off turns. Cut in butter until mixture begins to gather together, using on/off turns. Press crumbs into bottom of pan and up sides to ¾ inch from top; there should be no cracks. Refrigerate crust for at least 30 minutes.

For filling: Preheat oven to 325°F. Heat 1½ cups cream with chocolate in heavy medium saucepan over low heat until chocolate melts, stirring constantly. Cool 10 minutes.

Beat cream cheese with ¾ cup sugar until smooth. Beat in eggs one at a time until just combined. Beat in chocolate mixture, then remaining 10 tablespoons cherry liquid and vanilla. Pour into crust. Bake until outer 2 inches of cake are firm but center still moves slightly, about 1¼ hours (top may crack). Cool completely on rack. Top pan with paper towels and cover tightly with foil. Refrigerate cake for 1 to 2 days.

Remove foil, paper towels and pan sides from cake. Spread cherry topping over cake. Beat remaining 1 cup cream with 2 tablespoons sugar and kirsch to peaks. Spoon into center of cake. Top with chocolate curls if desired. (*Can be prepared 2 hours ahead and refrigerated.*) Let stand at room temperature for 15 minutes before serving.

*Available at Middle Eastern and specialty foods stores.

🍎 Cheesecake

Though it makes a spectacular dessert, the great thing about cheesecake is that it does not require any unusual or specialized cooking skills. Basically, the filling is a cream cheese custard that is "set" with eggs and by refrigeration. The cake bakes until it is barely set, because the internal heat will continue to cook and solidify the custard as it cools.

For best results, have all the ingredients at room temperature when you begin. This ensures that everything can be combined easily without a chance of overbeating and will yield a smooth custard "batter."

The shelves of any supermarket will provide most of the ingredients, but the cream cheese used deserves a special comment. For many years all brands were virtually identical. Recently, some manufacturers have reformulated the product so the cheese is soft and spreadable when taken directly from the refrigerator. These newer versions list vegetable gum or guar gum among the components. This type is not recommended for any of the recipes in this collection, since it may not firm the custard to the correct consistency. Read the labels carefully before purchasing.

Irish Coffee Cheesecake

Irish whiskey and espresso flavor the delicious filling, encased in an oatmeal cookie crust. As with most cheesecakes, if it is refrigerated overnight, the flavors will mellow.

10 servings

Oatmeal Crust
- ½ 12½-ounce package crisp oatmeal cookies
- 1 tablespoon firmly packed dark brown sugar
- ¼ teaspoon cinnamon
- 3½ tablespoons well-chilled unsalted butter, cut into small pieces

Coffee Filling
- 1½ pounds (24 ounces) cream cheese, room temperature
- 1 cup plus 2½ tablespoons firmly packed dark brown sugar
- 4 eggs, room temperature
- 2 tablespoons plus 2 teaspoons coffee liqueur
- ½ teaspoon vanilla
- 5 teaspoons instant espresso powder
- 7 tablespoons Irish whiskey

Topping
- ¾ teaspoon instant espresso powder
- ½ teaspoon sugar
- 1 tablespoon whipping cream
- 1½ cups well-chilled whipping cream
- 2 tablespoons sugar

Chocolate coffee beans

For crust: Preheat oven to 325°F. Lightly butter 9-inch springform pan. Finely grind cookies, sugar and cinnamon in processor. Add butter and process until crumbs hold together. Press into prepared pan, covering bottom and extending 1½ inches up sides. Bake until crust darkens slightly, about 8 minutes. Cool.

For filling: Preheat oven to 325°F. Blend cream cheese and sugar in processor until smooth, stopping occasionally to scrape down sides of bowl. Mix in 1 egg, liqueur and vanilla. Dissolve instant espresso powder in whiskey in large bowl. Stir in cheese mixture. Whisk in remaining 3 eggs one at a time. Pour filling into cooled crust. Bake until outer 2 inches of cake are firm and slightly puffed, about 45 minutes (center will appear moist and edges may crack slightly). Cool to room temperature on rack. Refrigerate until well chilled. Cover with plastic wrap and let mellow in refrigerator for 1 to 2 days.

For topping: Dissolve instant espresso powder and ½ teaspoon sugar in 1 tablespoon cream in small bowl. Beat 1½ cups cream and 2 tablespoons sugar in large bowl until peaks form. Fold in espresso mixture.

Remove plastic wrap and pan sides from cake. Spread top with whipped cream and garnish with coffee beans. (*Can be prepared 3 hours ahead and refrigerated.*) Let stand at room temperature 15 minutes before serving.

Eight Treasure Cheesecake

Another creation that benefits from mellowing time in the refrigerator.

8 servings

1 20-ounce can lichee nuts in heavy syrup
1 cup water
½ cup short-grain rice
2 slices fresh ginger (1 × ¼-inch rounds), peeled
Pinch of salt

1 pound (16 ounces) cream cheese, room temperature
½ cup sugar
4 eggs, room temperature
1 tablespoon fresh lemon juice
1 teaspoon vanilla
1 teaspoon almond extract
1 cup whipping cream

1 20-ounce can pineapple chunks in heavy syrup, drained
1 15-ounce can loquats in heavy syrup, drained
4 kiwis, peeled and sliced
2 tablespoons minced crystallized ginger

1 20-ounce can arbutus* or bing cherries in heavy syrup, drained
12 raisins, plumped in hot water 15 minutes and drained
12 blanched toasted almonds

Measure 1 cup lichee nut syrup (refrigerate fruit with remaining syrup) into heavy 2-quart saucepan. Add water, rice, ginger and salt. Bring to boil, stirring occasionally. Reduce heat, cover and simmer until rice absorbs all liquid and mixture is very thick, stirring frequently, about 35 minutes. Cover pan with paper towel, replace lid and cool rice for 35 minutes.

Preheat oven to 325°F. Butter 8-inch springform pan. Wrap outside thoroughly with foil to make watertight. Blend cream cheese and sugar in processor until smooth, stopping occasionally to scrape down sides of bowl. Mix in eggs one at a time. Blend in lemon juice, vanilla and almond extract. (If using standard-size processor, stir 1 cup cheese mixture into rice.) With machine running, pour cream through feed tube and blend until combined. Discard ginger from rice and stir cream cheese mixture into rice. Spoon into prepared pan. Set into larger pan. Pour simmering water into larger pan to depth of 1½ inches. Bake until top of cake is firm, about 65 minutes. Remove foil from pan and cool cake completely on rack. Refrigerate until chilled. Cover; refrigerate 2 to 3 days.

Drain reserved lichee nuts and discard syrup. Combine lichees with pineapple, loquats, kiwis and ginger in large bowl. Cover and refrigerate 1 hour.

Remove pan sides from cake. Set cake on platter. Arrange some of canned fruits in center. Sprinkle with raisins and almonds. Let stand at room temperature 20 minutes. Add arbutus to remaining fruits. Serve with cake.

*Arbutus is a small, dark red fruit available in cans at oriental markets.

Coconut Cream Cheesecake

Cream of coconut, fresh coconut and coconut liqueur combine for a rich and utterly delectable dessert.

12 servings

2½ cups grated fresh coconut
  1 cup whipping cream, scalded

Crust
  ⅔ cup all purpose flour
  5 tablespoons plus 1 teaspoon well-chilled butter, cut into ½-inch pieces
  4 teaspoons sugar

Coconut Filling
1¼ pounds (20 ounces) cream cheese, room temperature
1½ cups sugar

  4 eggs, room temperature
  2 egg yolks, room temperature
2½ tablespoons coconut liqueur
  1 teaspoon fresh lemon juice
  ½ teaspoon vanilla
  ½ teaspoon almond extract

  1 cup sour cream
  ¼ cup cream of coconut*
  ½ teaspoon coconut liqueur
     Lightly toasted coconut flakes

Puree coconut with hot cream in blender until finely shredded, about 4 minutes. Cool while preparing crust.

For crust: Preheat oven to 325°F. Butter bottom of 10-inch springform pan. Blend flour, butter and sugar until mixture begins to gather together. Press evenly into bottom of prepared pan. Bake until golden brown, about 25 minutes. Set on rack while preparing filling. Retain oven at 325°F.

For filling: Using electric mixer on low speed, beat cream cheese with sugar until blended. Mix in cooled coconut mixture. Blend in eggs and yolks one at a time. Mix in 2½ tablespoons liqueur, lemon juice, vanilla and almond extract. Pour into prepared crust. Return to oven and bake until sides of cake are dry and center no longer moves when shaken, about 1 hour. Let cake cool on rack until depression forms in center, about 35 minutes.

Preheat oven to 325°F. Mix sour cream, cream of coconut and remaining ½ teaspoon coconut liqueur. Spread atop cake. Bake 10 minutes to set topping. Cool completely on rack. Refrigerate until cake is well chilled, about 4 hours. Cover tightly and refrigerate 1 day to mellow flavors. (*Can be prepared 3 days ahead.*) Spread coconut flakes in 1-inch band around rim.

*Available at liquor stores and specialty foods section of some supermarkets.

Russian Cheesecake

An opulently rich fruit- and nut-studded version of the classic Russian dessert paskha.

10 to 12 servings

  1 pound (4 sticks) unsalted butter, room temperature
  2 pounds (32 ounces) cream cheese, room temperature
  3 egg yolks

1½ cups sifted powdered sugar
  2 teaspoons vanilla
  ¾ cup chopped mixed dried apricots, dates and prunes
  ¾ cup chopped walnuts

Line 2-quart earthenware flowerpot with double thickness of cheesecloth, leaving 3-inch overhang. Cream butter in large bowl of electric mixer. Beat in cream cheese a little at a time on low speed until mixture is just creamy; do not overmix. Beat in yolks one at a time. Mix in powdered sugar and vanilla. Fold in dried fruit and walnuts. Spoon filling into prepared flowerpot and level top with spatula. Fold cheesecloth over top. Place on rimmed dish and refrigerate overnight.

To serve, gently pull cheesecloth to loosen cake from pot (cake should be very firm). Invert cake onto platter; peel away cheesecloth. Cut into thin slices with warm knife.

Linzertorte Cheesecake

This stunning cake has an almond crust made from dough that is sliced like refrigerator cookies for easier handling. Cottage cheese adds creaminess to the rum-laced filling.

10 servings

Almond Crust
- ³/₄ cup unblanched almonds, toasted
- 1 tablespoon sugar
- 1¹/₄ cups all purpose flour
- ¹/₂ cup sugar
- 4 teaspoons grated lemon peel
- ³/₄ teaspoon cinnamon
- ¹/₂ teaspoon salt
- ¹/₄ teaspoon ground cloves
- ¹/₄ teaspoon baking powder
- ¹/₈ teaspoon ground ginger
- 10 tablespoons (1¹/₄ sticks) well-chilled unsalted butter, cut into ¹/₂-inch pieces
- 1 egg
- 1 teaspoon vanilla
- ¹/₂ teaspoon almond extract

Filling
- 1 pound large-curd cottage cheese
- ¹/₂ cup sugar
- ¹/₄ cup (¹/₂ stick) unsalted butter, room temperature
- 8 ounces cream cheese, cut into 1-inch pieces, room temperature
- ¹/₂ cup sour cream
- 2 eggs
- 1 egg yolk
- 2 tablespoons dark rum
- 1 teaspoon vanilla
- ¹/₂ teaspoon fresh lemon juice

- 1 egg blended with 1 teaspoon cornstarch (glaze)

- 1 egg white, beaten to blend

Raspberry Topping
- 1 10-ounce package frozen raspberries in syrup, thawed and drained
- ¹/₄ cup seedless red raspberry jam

For crust: Finely grind almonds with 1 tablespoon sugar in processor. Set aside. Blend flour with next 7 ingredients in processor. Cut in butter until mixture resembles coarse meal, using on/off turns. Add egg, vanilla and almond extract and blend until dough just begins to gather together (do not form ball). Transfer to medium bowl and work in ³/₄ cup nut mixture using rubber spatula. Reserve remaining nuts. Form dough into 12-inch log. Wrap and refrigerate at least 4 hours. (*Can be prepared 3 days ahead.*)

Halve 36 sour cherries from preserves (reserve remainder for garnish). Rinse and pat dry. Combine with apricots and liqueur in small dish. Cover and let soak several hours or overnight, stirring occasionally.

Preheat oven to 350°F. Butter bottom of 9-inch springform pan. Blend flour, ¹/₄ cup butter and sugar in processor until mixture begins to gather together. Press evenly into bottom of prepared pan. Bake until golden brown, about 18 minutes. Cool on rack while preparing chocolate layer. Retain oven at 350°F.

For chocolate layer: Blend all ingredients except minichips in processor until smooth, stopping occasionally to scrape down sides of work bowl. Stir in minichips. Pour filling into crust. Return to oven and bake until center of layer no longer moves when shaken, 23 to 25 minutes. Cool on rack while preparing almond layer. Retain oven temperature at 350°F.

For almond layer: Puree first 3 ingredients in processor until smooth. Add remaining ingredients and blend until smooth, stopping occasionally to scrape down sides of work bowl. Carefully spoon mixture atop chocolate layer. Return to oven and bake until center of layer no longer moves when shaken, about 26 minutes. Cool on rack while preparing fruit layer. Retain oven at 350°F.

For fruit layer: Puree cheese, eggs, sugar, fruit peels and food coloring in processor until smooth, stopping occasionally to scrape down sides of work bowl. Blend in cherry mixture using on/off turns. Carefully spoon atop almond layer. Return to oven and bake until center of layer no longer moves when shaken, about 28 minutes. Cool completely on rack. Refrigerate cake until well chilled. Cover with plastic and refrigerate 2 days to mellow flavors.

Transfer cake to platter. Remove wrap and pan sides. Scrape sides to reveal 3 layers, using knife. Spoon whipped cream into pastry bag fitted with medium star tip. Pipe cream in rosettes around rim. Set remaining cherries atop rosettes. Let stand at room temperature 20 minutes before serving.

For filling: Drain cottage cheese in strainer, pressing with back of spoon. Wrap in kitchen towel and press to dry. Blend sugar and butter in processor 10 seconds. Add cottage cheese and puree until smooth, stopping occasionally to scrape down sides of work bowl. Mix in cream cheese, sour cream, eggs, yolk, rum, vanilla and lemon juice until smooth. Cover and refrigerate at least 6 hours. (*Filling can be prepared 3 days ahead.*)

To assemble: Butter bottom of 9-inch springform pan. Cut dough in half and return 1 half to refrigerator. Slice remainder into 1/8-inch-thick rounds. Press into prepared pan, covering bottom and extending 1 inch up sides to form crust. Freeze 20 minutes.

Preheat oven to 425°F. Line crust with buttered foil and fill with dried beans or rice. Bake until crust is golden brown, about 20 minutes. Remove beans and foil. Brush crust with egg glaze and sprinkle with reserved nuts. Reduce oven temperature to 350°F. Bake crust 5 minutes. Cool slightly.

Stir filling and spoon into crust. Bake until center no longer moves when shaken, about 50 minutes. Remove pan sides. Cool cake completely on rack. Increase oven to 425°F.

Line baking sheet with double layer of parchment. Place 9-inch springform pan rim upside down atop parchment. Slice remaining dough into 1/4-inch-thick rounds, then cut into 3/8-inch-thick strips. Overlap strip ends and roll into 9 × 1/4-inch ropes. Arrange 8 ropes in lattice pattern within pan rim. Arrange remaining ropes around inside edge of pan to form border, pressing ends together. Freeze 5 minutes.

Brush lattice with egg white. Bake until golden brown, 16 to 18 minutes. Gently remove pan rim and transfer parchment and lattice to rack. Cool.

Cut cake crust level with filling if necessary. Refrigerate cake 3 hours. Replace pan rim, cover cake with plastic and refrigerate overnight.

For topping: Press berries through fine sieve, discarding seeds. Simmer 1/4 cup puree with jam in heavy small saucepan until thick, about 3 minutes. Brush in 1/2-inch border around top edge of cake. Slide lattice atop cake. Spoon remaining topping between lattice strips. Let cool 1 hour. Refrigerate cake for 3 hours before serving.

Raspberry Cheesecake Japonaise

A glamorous chocolate-frosted cheesecake with the surprise of meringue.

16 servings

Meringue Crusts
  6 ounces almonds, toasted
  4 ounces hazelnuts, toasted
  1½ cups sugar
  1½ tablespoons cornstarch
  9 egg whites, room temperature

Cheesecake
  18 ounces cream cheese, room temperature
  ¾ cup sugar
  4 eggs, room temperature
  6 tablespoons raspberry liqueur
  ¾ teaspoon vanilla

Frosting
  8 ounces cream cheese, room temperature
  1 cup (2 sticks) unsalted butter, room temperature
  3 tablespoons sour cream
  1 teaspoon vanilla
  5 ounces semisweet chocolate, melted and cooled
  12 ounces fresh or thawed and drained frozen raspberries

For meringue: Preheat oven to 275°F. Line 2 baking sheets with parchment paper; butter and flour paper. Draw two 9-inch circles on 1 sheet. Finely grind almonds and hazelnuts with ½ cup sugar and cornstarch in processor. Beat whites with ½ cup sugar to firm peaks. Fold remaining ½ cup sugar and ground nut mixture into whites. Spoon meringue into pastry bag fitted with ½-inch plain tip. Pipe some of meringue over 1 circle on prepared sheet, beginning in center and spiraling outward to edge. Repeat over second circle. Pipe remaining meringue in strips onto second prepared sheet. Bake until meringues are dry and barely colored, about 1 hour. Remove from paper and cool completely on rack. (*Can be prepared 1 day ahead. Store in container at room temperature.*)

For cheesecake: Preheat oven to 350°F. Butter 9-inch round cake pan. Line with parchment paper; butter and flour paper. Using electric mixer, beat cream cheese and sugar until smooth. Beat in eggs one at a time. Blend in liqueur and vanilla. Turn batter into prepared pan, spreading evenly. Set pan on rimmed baking sheet. Pour about ½ inch of water onto sheet. Bake until tester inserted in center comes out clean, about 30 minutes. Turn off oven. Cool cake 15 minutes with door slightly ajar. Remove from oven and cool to room temperature. Cover and refrigerate at least 1 hour.

For frosting: Using electric mixer, beat cream cheese and butter until smooth. Mix in sour cream and vanilla. Blend in chocolate. Divide frosting in half. Set aside 16 raspberries. Fold remaining raspberries into half of chocolate frosting.

To assemble: Trim meringue rounds if necessary to diameter of 9 inches. Set 1 round on platter. Spread with layer of chocolate-raspberry frosting. Carefully invert cheesecake onto round. Spread with layer of chocolate-raspberry frosting. Top with second meringue round. Spread top and sides of cake with thin layer of chocolate frosting. Using sharp knife, mark off 16 slices on top of cake. Trim meringue strips even with height of cake. Press strips into frosting around cake with sides touching. Spoon remaining chocolate frosting into pastry bag fitted with star tip. Pipe decorative border around top edge of cake. Refrigerate cake until firm. Let stand at room temperature 2 hours. Just before serving, top each rosette with 1 raspberry.

Apple-Bavarian Torte

6 servings

Vanilla Crust
- 1 cup all purpose flour
- ⅓ cup sugar
- ½ teaspoon vanilla
- ½ cup (1 stick) well-chilled butter, cut into small pieces

Cream Cheese Filling
- 1 pound (16 ounces) cream cheese, room temperature
- ½ cup sugar
- 1 teaspoon vanilla
- 2 eggs, room temperature

Apple Topping
- 2 large tart green apples, peeled, cored and thinly sliced
- ¼ cup sugar
- ½ teaspoon cinnamon
- ½ teaspoon vanilla
- ⅓ cup coarsely chopped walnuts

For crust: Preheat oven to 350°F. Combine flour, sugar and vanilla in medium bowl. Cut in butter using pastry blender or 2 knives until mixture resembles coarse meal. Press into bottom and sides of 10-inch springform pan. Bake until golden, about 5 minutes. Cool to room temperature. Increase oven to 450°F.

For filling: Beat cream cheese, sugar and vanilla with electric mixer until smooth. Beat in eggs one at a time. Spoon into crust.

For topping: Mix apples, sugar, cinnamon and vanilla. Spoon over cream cheese layer, spreading evenly. Sprinkle with walnuts. Bake 15 minutes. Reduce oven temperature to 350°F. Continue baking until tester inserted in center comes out clean, about 45 minutes. Cool torte completely in pan on rack. Refrigerate. Let stand at room temperature for 30 minutes before serving.

Chocolate Cheese Torte

This must be prepared one day ahead.

10 to 12 servings

Pastry
1½ cups unbleached all purpose flour
 2 tablespoons sugar
⅛ teaspoon grated lemon peel
 Pinch of salt
½ cup plus 2 tablespoons (1¼ sticks) unsalted butter, cut into ½-inch pieces, room temperature
 1 egg yolk
 1 teaspoon water
½ teaspoon vanilla

Chocolate-Cheese Filling
5½ ounces semisweet chocolate, coarsely chopped
½ cup (1 stick) unsalted butter, coarsely chopped
 1 ounce unsweetened chocolate, coarsely chopped

¾ cup sugar
 3 eggs, room temperature

¾ cup pecans, very finely ground
 3 tablespoons all purpose flour
 2 cups Topfen* (fresh cream cheese or half cream cheese and half pot cheese can be substituted)
¾ cup sour cream
 2 teaspoons finely ground espresso beans
½ teaspoon cinnamon
⅛ teaspoon grated lemon peel
⅛ teaspoon salt

¾ cup whipping cream
 3 tablespoons powdered sugar
 1 teaspoon vanilla
 1 ounce semisweet chocolate (garnish)

For pastry: Combine flour, sugar, lemon peel and salt in large bowl. Work in butter until crumbly. Beat yolk, water and vanilla to blend. Add to flour mixture and blend until smooth. Press about half of dough evenly into bottom of 9-inch springform pan. Roll remaining dough into a rope about 1 inch in diameter. Coil rope around base of pan. Dust fingertips lightly with flour and press dough evenly up sides (about 2½ inches high), being careful to make top edge very straight and even. (If necessary, trim edges with knife.) Gently press edge down to form slight lip. Using blunt side of knife, indent edge of dough at ½-inch intervals, forming scallops. Freeze for at least 1 hour.

Preheat oven to 375°F. Line pastry shell with foil. Fill with dried beans, rice or pie weights. Bake 20 minutes. Remove beans and foil and continue baking until lightly browned, 15 to 20 more minutes (if bottom of pastry begins to puff, pierce with knife to allow steam to escape). Cool in pan on rack.

For filling: Preheat oven to 350°F. Melt 5½ ounces semisweet chocolate with butter and unsweetened chocolate in heavy large saucepan over hot water, stirring occasionally until smooth.

Meanwhile, beat sugar and eggs in large bowl of electric mixer until pale yellow and slowly dissolving ribbon forms when beaters are lifted, about 7 minutes. Mix ground pecans with flour. Stir topfen, sour cream, espresso beans, cinnamon, lemon peel, salt, melted chocolate and flour mixture into eggs. Pour into pastry shell, smoothing surface with spatula. Bake until edges begin to puff (center will not be set), 30 to 40 minutes. Cool on rack. Refrigerate overnight.

Whip cream with powdered sugar and vanilla to stiff peaks. Spoon cream into pastry bag fitted with decorative tip. Remove sides of springform. Transfer torte to platter. Pipe rosettes of cream around torte rim. Using vegetable peeler, shave chocolate onto waxed paper. Refrigerate until chilled. Using chilled metal spatula, sprinkle chocolate shavings atop rosettes. Serve torte at room temperature.

*Topfen
(Pot Cheese)

This is a fresh curd similar to our cottage cheese. In France, pot cheese is cooked at a lower temperature for a shorter period of time, resulting in a softer, slightly smoother-textured cheese known as fromage blanc. *It is usually eaten with cream and sugar or used to prepare the popular dessert,* coeur à la crème. *Quark is a creamier version and can be used interchangeably with Topfen as long as the amount of liquid in the recipe is changed accordingly (see* Variations*). This recipe can be halved.*

Makes about 4 cups

4 quarts homogenized milk	
1 cup fresh cultured buttermilk,	room temperature

Warm milk to 85°F to 90°F in large saucepan or large metal bowl set over boiling water; do not let pan touch water. Blend into buttermilk. Set aside in warm place (80°F to 90°F) until pleasantly sour-tasting curd is formed, about 24 hours. (*To assure that milk is properly thickened, insert knife into curds at an angle and lift up. Curds should break away cleanly from knife.*)

Using long knife, cut down through curds, then across through curds, forming about 1-inch cubes (a wire also works well for cutting the horizontal layers). Place over simmering water over low heat. Slowly heat curds to 120°F to 130°F, gently stirring occasionally to distribute heat evenly. Cook until curds and whey look separated, 20 to 30 minutes, stirring gently 3 or 4 times and maintaining temperature at 120°F to 130°F. Let mixture cool to room temperature.

Line colander with several layers of moistened cheesecloth. Using slotted or mesh spoon or small strainer, carefully scoop curds into colander (curds are very delicate and should be kept as compact as possible). Tie corners of cheesecloth around wooden spoon handle. Suspend curds over bowl. Let drain until completely dry, 6 to 8 hours. Transfer to airtight container and refrigerate until ready to use. (*Can be prepared up to 1 week ahead.*)

Variations:
For fromage blanc, cook curds at 105°F to 110°F for 10 to 15 minutes. For quark, stir crème fraîche into dry curds.

Almond Cheesecake

12 servings

Crust
1½ cups graham cracker crumbs
¼ cup (½ stick) butter, melted
2 tablespoons sugar
1 teaspoon all purpose flour

Filling
2 pounds (32 ounces) cream cheese, room temperature
1 cup sugar
2 eggs, beaten to blend
1 teaspoon vanilla
1 teaspoon almond extract

2 cups sour cream
¾ cup sugar
¾ teaspoon almond extract
½ teaspoon fresh lemon juice

For crust: Preheat oven to 350°F. Combine crumbs, melted butter, sugar and flour in medium bowl and mix thoroughly. Pat mixture onto bottom and sides of 10-inch springform pan. Bake 5 minutes. Let cool. Turn off oven.

For filling: Beat cream cheese, 1 cup sugar, eggs, vanilla and 1 teaspoon almond extract at low speed in large bowl of electric mixer until smooth. Pour into crust. Place in oven; turn temperature back to 350°F. Bake until firm and set, about 30 minutes.

Combine remaining ingredients in medium bowl and blend well. Using rubber spatula, spread mixture over cheesecake to within ½ inch of edge. Bake 8 minutes. Cool completely, about 2 hours. Refrigerate overnight. Just before serving, remove springform; set cake on platter.

Cheesecake can be refrigerated up to 1 week.

Spumoni Cheesecake

Festive fare for an Italian party.

12 servings

1 10-ounce jar sour cherry preserves
¼ cup diced dried apricots (¼-inch pieces)
1 tablespoon orange liqueur

½ cup all purpose flour
¼ cup (½ stick) well-chilled butter, cut into ½-inch pieces
1 tablespoon sugar

Chocolate Layer
11 ounces cream cheese, cut into 1-inch pieces, room temperature
2 medium eggs, room temperature
½ cup sugar
4 teaspoons unsweetened cocoa powder (preferably Dutch process)
1 tablespoon chocolate syrup
½ teaspoon vanilla
¼ cup semisweet chocolate minichips

Almond Layer
3 tablespoons almond paste
3 tablespoons whipping cream
¼ teaspoon almond extract

11 ounces cream cheese, cut into 1-inch pieces, room temperature
2 medium eggs, room temperature
½ cup sugar

Fruit Layer
11 ounces cream cheese, cut into 1-inch pieces, room temperature
2 medium eggs, room temperature
½ cup sugar
1 teaspoon grated orange peel
1 teaspoon grated lemon peel
5 drops red food coloring

½ cup whipping cream, whipped to peaks

Halve 36 sour cherries from preserves (reserve remainder for garnish). Rinse and pat dry. Combine with apricots and liqueur in small dish. Cover and let soak several hours or overnight, stirring occasionally.

Preheat oven to 350°F. Butter bottom of 9-inch springform pan. Blend flour, ¼ cup butter and sugar in processor until mixture begins to gather together. Press evenly into bottom of prepared pan. Bake until golden brown, about 18 minutes. Cool on rack while preparing chocolate layer. Retain oven at 350°F.

For chocolate layer: Blend all ingredients except mini-chips in processor until smooth, stopping occasionally to scrape down sides of work bowl. Stir in mini-chips. Pour filling into crust. Return to oven and bake until center of layer no longer moves when shaken, 23 to 25 minutes. Cool on rack while preparing almond layer. Retain oven temperature at 350°F.

For almond layer: Puree first 3 ingredients in processor until smooth. Add remaining ingredients and blend until smooth, stopping occasionally to scrape down sides of work bowl. Carefully spoon mixture atop chocolate layer. Return to oven and bake until center of layer no longer moves when shaken, about 26 minutes. Cool on rack while preparing fruit layer. Retain oven at 350°F.

For fruit layer: Puree cheese, eggs, sugar, fruit peels and food coloring in processor until smooth, stopping occasionally to scrape down sides of work bowl. Blend in cherry mixture using on/off turns. Carefully spoon atop almond layer. Return to oven and bake until center of layer no longer moves when shaken, about 28 minutes. Cool completely on rack. Refrigerate cake until well chilled. Cover with plastic and refrigerate 2 days to mellow flavors.

Transfer cake to platter. Remove wrap and pan sides. Scrape sides to reveal 3 layers, using knife. Spoon whipped cream into pastry bag fitted with medium star tip. Pipe cream in rosettes around rim. Set remaining cherries atop rosettes. Let stand at room temperature 20 minutes before serving.

Butterscotch Phyllo Cheesecake

8 to 10 servings

½ cup raisins
3 tablespoons dark rum

Crust
½ cup (1 stick) butter
⅓ cup sugar
1 egg
1½ cups all purpose flour

4 phyllo pastry sheets
¼ cup (½ stick) butter, melted

Filling
4 8-ounce packages cream cheese, room temperature
½ cup sugar

2 tablespoons all purpose flour
4 eggs, room temperature
1 egg yolk, room temperature
½ cup whipping cream

Butterscotch Sauce
5 tablespoons butter
1 cup firmly packed light brown sugar
⅓ cup whipping cream
2 tablespoons dark corn syrup
1 teaspoon vanilla

Soak raisins in rum overnight.

For crust: Cream butter with sugar until light and fluffy. Beat in egg. Gradually mix in flour. Cover dough and chill 2 hours.

Grease and flour bottom and sides of 10-inch springform pan. Roll dough out on lightly floured surface to thickness of ⅛ to ¼ inch. Cut out 10-inch circle. Fit dough into bottom of prepared pan.

Brush each phyllo sheet with some of melted butter. Arrange sheets buttered side up over dough in pan, covering bottom and sides (allow overhang to drape over sides). Drain raisins. Sprinkle over phyllo.

For filling: Preheat oven to 325°F. Beat cream cheese with sugar until smooth. Add flour and mix until smooth. Beat in eggs and yolk one at a time. Add cream and stir just to incorporate. Pour into crust. Fold overhanging phyllo over filling, separating ends and pulling upward to form rough, jagged "crown." Bake until firm, about 70 minutes. Cool cake completely.

For sauce: Melt butter in heavy small saucepan. Stir in brown sugar, cream and corn syrup. Increase heat and bring to boil. Remove sauce from heat and blend in vanilla.

Place cake on large platter. Drizzle sauce over top of cake and allow to pool around bottom. To serve, cut cake into wedges. Pass any remaining sauce separately.

❧ Index

❦ *Credits and Acknowledgments*

The following people contributed the recipes included in this book:

Jean Anderson
Nancy Barocci
Beggar's Banquet, East Lansing, Michigan
Nic and Nancy Boghosian
Anita Borghese
Flo Braker
Café at Bon Appétit, Philadelphia, Pennsylvania
Cafe Metro, Louisville, Kentucky
Irena Chalmers
Dailey's Restaurant & Bar, Atlanta, Georgia
Diane Darrow
Deirdre Davis
Diane Dexter
D'Imperio's, Pittsburgh, Pennsylvania
Enjolie, Dallas, Texas
Olivia Erschen
Joe Famularo
Michel Fitoussi
Helen Fletcher
Robert and Shelley Friedman
Shelly Gillette
Peggy Glass
Mary Green
Freddi Greenberg
Pamela Grosscup
The Holly Hotel, Holly, Michigan
Hotel Palácio dos Seteais, Sintra, Portugal
Hyeholde Restaurant, Coraopolis, Pennsylvania

Liisa Jasinski
Cyndee Kannenberg
Shari Karney
Lynne Kasper
Le Bocage, Watertown, Massachusetts
L'Ermitage, Los Angeles, Calfornia
Faye Levy
John Loring
Abby Mandel
Tom Maresca
Linda Marino
The Market Place, Asheville, North Carolina
The Marlborough Hotel, Ipswich, England
Lydie Marshall
Sunny Marx
Paula McDevitt
Carmela Meely
Miriam Miller
Jinx Morgan
Selma Morrow
Anton Mosimann
Donna Nordin
Beatrice Ojakangas
Old Lyme Inn, Lyme, Connecticut
The Peasant, Atlanta, Georgia
Péché Mignon, Huntington, New York
Pat Pepe
Richard Perry
Pilou Restaurant, Sonoma, California
Jean-Jacques Rachou
Restaurant Le Beaujolais, Banff, Alberta

Rex—Il Ristorante, Los Angeles, California
Michel Richard
Ristorante da Luciano, San Francisco, California
Jacky Robert
Betty Rosbottom
Rudi's Big Indian, Big Indian, New York
Sacks Cafe, Anchorage, Alaska
Carol Samuelo
Jimmy Schmidt
Dieter Schorner
Sebastian's, London, Ontario
Gillian Servais
Nancy Silverton
Douglas Spingler
Bonnie Stern
Marimar Torres
Michele Urvater
Nancy Ellard Vass
Charlotte Walker
Jan Weimer
Anne Willan

Additional text was supplied by:
Olivia Erschen and Charlotte Walker, *Charlottes;* Faye Levy, *Crème Anglaise;* Selma Morrow, *Cheesecake;* Jan Weimer, *Mousses*

The Knapp Press
is a wholly owned subsidiary of
KNAPP COMMUNICATIONS CORPORATION.

Composition by Publisher's Typography

This book is set in Sabon, a face designed by Jan Teischold in 1967 and based on early fonts engraved by Garamond and Granjon.